GENDER PERFORMATIVITY IN SPORTS AND PHYSICAL EDUCATION

A link to access additional online resources is provided at:
https://doi.org/10.18848/978-1-963049-23-7/CGP

SPORT & SOCIETY POCKETBOOK TEACHING SERIES

The **Sport and Society Pocketbook Teaching Series** aims to introduce students and a general readership to relevant topics, theories, and concepts within sport history and sport sociology. The topics will vary but are united in their purpose to serve as an accessible alternative to generic textbook offerings or academic research monographs. We hope that the shorter and more accessible pocketbook format of the series will mean that each book can be read in an hour or two on a quiet evening or while commuting on a bus or train. This aligns with our ethos of accessibility in scholarly communication.

Books in the series can be accessed in print and electronic formats. In addition, and in parallel to both editions, each title will be accompanied by an online repository where additional learning and teaching resources are provided. The electronic platform for the series will include links to recent and significant research articles, visual materials, podcasts, lectures, and more, thus securing ongoing relevance by providing new and engaging resources and perspectives aligned with the topic of each book.

This series is for teachers, learners, and individuals with an interest in sports alike.

Dr. Jörg Krieger (Aarhus University, Denmark)
Dr. April Henning (Heriot-Watt University, United Kingdom)
Dr. Lindsay Parks Pieper (University of Lynchburg, United States)
Dr. Jesper Andreasson (Linnaeus University, Sweden)

GENDER PERFORMATIVITY IN SPORTS AND PHYSICAL EDUCATION

HÅKAN LARSSON

First published in 2024
as part of the Sport & Society Book Imprint
doi: 10.18848/978-1-963049-23-7/CGP (Full Book)

Common Ground Research Networks
2001 South First Street, Suite 202
University of Illinois Research Park
Champaign, IL
61820

Copyright © Håkan Larsson, 2024

All rights reserved. Apart from fair dealing for the purposes of study, research, criticism or review as permitted under the applicable copyright legislation, no part of this book may be reproduced by any process without written permission from the publisher.

Library of Congress Cataloging-in-Publication Data

Names: Larsson, Håkan, 1967- author.
Title: Gender performativity in sports and physical education / Håkan Larsson.
Description: Champaign, IL : Common Ground Research Networks, 2024. | Series: Sport and society pocketbook teaching series | Includes bibliographical references. | Summary: "The purpose of Gender Performativity in Sports and Physical Education is to explore a perspective of gender called gender performativity. The notion of gender performativity was coined by Judith Butler in the early 1990s. It starts from the idea that gender is something people do rather than something they are. Such a perspective offers new ways of understanding gender, and therefore also gender equity, in sports and physical education. It offers new ways to think about how inequitable practices can change. Empirical illustrations of gender performativity in sports and physical education are mainly drawn from Håkan Larsson's thirty-year research on the matter, but connections are also made to other research in the field"-- Provided by publisher.
Identifiers: LCCN 2024004366 (print) | LCCN 2024004367 (ebook) | ISBN 9781963049220 (pbk : alk. paper) | ISBN 9781963049237 (pdf) | ISBN 9781963049244 (epub)
Subjects: LCSH: Sports--Sex differences. | Physical education and training--Sex differences. | Gender identity in sports. | Sex differences (Psychology)--Social aspects. | Sports--Physiological aspects.
Classification: LCC GV706.47 .L37 2024 (print) | LCC GV706.47 (ebook) | DDC 796.081--dc23/eng/20240301
LC record available at https://lccn.loc.gov/2024004366
LC ebook record available at https://lccn.loc.gov/2024004367

Cover Photo Credit: © Håkan Larsson

TABLE OF CONTENTS

An Introduction	13
The Origins of Sports and Physical Education	29
Theorising Gender. Outlining Gender Performativity	47
Gender Performativity in Sports	67
Gender Performativity in Physical Education	85
LGBTQI+ Issues in Sports and Physical Education	103
Conclusions And the Way Forward	121
References	125

CHAPTER 1

Gender Performativity in Sports and Physical Education. An Introduction

Introduction

Gender affects sport and physical education in numerous ways. Gendered practices are, for example, the division into a male and a female competition class in sports or school classes with girls or boys in physical education. Such divisions may seem 'natural' and unproblematic and are required to promote gender equity in sports and physical education. However, they may also have unintended consequences that negatively affect gender equity. The line between the genders is not as clear and unambiguous as one might first think. Moreover, gender segregation creates strong ideas about how girls and boys, men and women, 'are,' which adversely affects people's ability to make their own choices, regardless of ideas about gender.

The purpose of this book is to explore a perspective of gender called *gender performativity* as an alternative to the tendency in sports and physical education to think about gender in terms of 'naturalness' and how girls and boys, men and women 'are.' The notion of gender performativity starts from the idea that gender is something people *do* rather than something they *are*. Such a perspective offers new ways of understanding gender, and therefore also gender equity, in sports and physical education. It offers new ways to think about how inequitable practices can change.

The notion of gender performativity was developed as a tool to challenge taken for granted ideas about gender, gender differences, and sexual orientation, which have contributed to reproducing power orders where men are valued more than women, where heterosexuality is valued more than other sexualities, and where cisgender (cis) people are valued more than transgender (trans) and intersex people. Before I delve deeper into the notion of gender performativity, I will say a few words about myself and why I am interested in questions about gender in sports and physical education.

Who am I – What am I?

According to a widespread research ideal, researchers should strive to relate objectively to, or detached from, what is being studied. My impression is that some researchers therefore believe that they must suppress all thoughts about their own relationship to the research interest. This is unfortunate and probably leads to even greater bias than if the researcher thoroughly articulated this relationship. Why am I interested in questions about gender in sports and physical education? What does gender equity mean to me? Such questions are not easy to answer simply because you did not think about 'why?' when you developed the interest. Nevertheless, a topic like gender can hardly be treated strictly objectively by anyone. Regardless of who you are, man, woman, trans, straight, gay, … you are always in some form of relationship with *gender norms*, those tacit assumptions about what it means to be human, including the assumption that people come in only two versions, which are also the premise of sexual attraction. If you identify as being either a man or a woman, and if you are also attracted to the 'opposite sex,' then probably gender norms work to your advantage. This means that you are less inclined to bother about them, or even detect them. It is often not until you act against the norms that you discover their power. Then, they may make you feel awkward, frustrated, irritated ... And what is worse, they may prevent you from doing what you aspire to most of all. You may even be subjected to violence and harassment. Pedagogically, this means that if you want to know more about gender norms, *try to break them*, and see what happens!

I was born in May 1967 as the second son of Britt and Nils-Eric. Almost five years earlier, at ages 20 and 25 respectively, they had their first-born son, Mats. My father, who was brought up in the countryside in southernmost Sweden, and himself a son of a construction worker and a housewife, spent seven years in primary school before he entered working life in his teens. After various sorts of manual labour, including being a fisherman at the time of my birth, he ended up working as a seller at a hardware store. My mother, who was a city girl, daughter of a rubber factory worker and a housewife, spent four years in primary school followed by another five years in junior secondary school. She planned to enter senior secondary school at age 16, which was a major financial commitment during the 1950s. However, after having a summer job at the local pharmacy, she decided to stay there – for 45 years.

As a little brother, I was little in several ways. While my big brother was somewhat stout, very practical, and loved to work outdoors, I was thin and considered delicate, and preferred to read and play indoors. In some of the few photos that exist from my childhood, I look feminine compared to my brother. Feet and legs together; head tilted slightly to the side with a somewhat uncertain look. In some pictures of myself as a two-year old, I have long, curly, linen-coloured hair. I remember distinctly that I was convinced that I was actually a girl for some time afterwards. In several ways, I now believe that I did not live up to many of the gender norms associated with a working-class boy. However, in those early years, during the 1960s and 70s, gender norms and the cultural imperative to identify unequivocally as someone, or something, i.e., boy, girl, trans, might not have been as important as it would become later. Moreover, during the 1980s, I discovered sports and grew to become 6'5" tall. Initially, I played football (soccer), but at age fourteen, I encountered track and field, which I enjoyed because boys and girls practiced together. I enjoyed the atmosphere of the mixed gender athletics club more than the one in the gender homogeneous football club.

Despite growing quite tall and developing a rather athletic body, in my teens I still felt difficult to live up to some gender norms, especially ones about courting girls. Yes, I fell in love with girls, but I could not figure out what I should do about it. I went through my teens without ever 'being with' a girl. At one point while attending upper secondary school, my grandmother, who was curious and candid, asked me: "you're not gay, are you?" I have often wondered about grandmother's reaction if I had replied: "yes, I am!" But what does it matter? I did not identify as gay, and at the same time I cannot imagine that my kind-hearted grandmother would not have accepted it if I did. Possibly, experiences like these lie behind why I developed such a deep interest in exploring gender norms. What are gender ideologies? What are their consequences? How can they be affected and changed?

Voilà – a curiosity about gender norms which is based, at least to some extent, on an inability to do gender correctly, can be experienced also by a self-identified heterosexual man, now in middle age. By the way, I belong to a social category that is often perceived to be the most advantaged in society – and rightly so, I must confess. This social category is sometimes considered to be notoriously unable to come to grips with the challenges that exist for other, less privileged, groups of people. I can recount several occasions where I have been advantaged by being a straight man, despite my own struggles. For example, I remember well, as a young lecturer in teacher education, how my female colleagues repeatedly complained about how upset students could become when feminism and gender equity were discussed in class. "I don't get those responses," I exclaimed in surprise. It was hard to accept that the students' greater benevolence towards me could be because I was a man and as such, I was not considered to 'speak in my own favour.' The example illustrates, however, how 'the man,' or more precisely, the white, middle-class, heterosexual man, is, perhaps implicitly, regarded as the *general* human being. While a white, middle-class, heterosexual man can represent humanity in general (as in Leonardo da Vincis *Homo Universalis*), a woman, a Black person, or a gay person is always a specific human being: woman, black or gay. Consequently, albeit also mostly implicitly, while (white, middle-class, heterosexual) men are assumed to be able to take an objective stance on reality, all other social categories are assumed to be subjective.

Many progressive men with similar backgrounds as myself have expressed frustration at how they feel misunderstood about their views on gender; how people project stereotypical gender norms onto them, even if they see themselves as progressive. Yes, I have experienced it myself, but I realise that it is a cheap price to pay for someone who can live up to expectations of normalcy. Instead of letting myself get overly frustrated, I have tried my best to approach the matter with curiosity: here is an opportunity to learn something new!

Perspectives of Gender and Sexuality

Now, let me return to the issue of gender, which is the central concept in the book. In conventional terms it refers to the social, cultural, psychological, and behavioural aspects of being a man or a woman. Gender is sometimes treated as synonymous with sex, which is more linked to the biological aspects of being a man or a woman. This division between 'the social' and 'the natural,' or between what is seen as given by, for example, genetics, hormones, biology, etc., and what is affected by cultural and social norms, can also be found in the different gender ideologies identified by sport sociologist Michael Messner (2011), who outlined four overall 'ideologies' of gender.

In the first perspective, which Messner called *hard essentialism*, there is an absolute division between the genders, where men are seen as 'naturally' masculine while women are seen as 'naturally' feminine. This view of gender dominated Western societies during the 19th and 20th centuries. A reaction against the categorical view of gender emerged in the 1970s, when an alternative perspective surfaced, which Messner calls *binary constructionism*. This perspective challenged the notion that gender is strictly 'natural,' but is affected by norms that are the result of social processes. However, to some people this second perspective did not challenge enough the beliefs that gender difference is the result of nature. Thus, more alternative perspectives were formulated in the late 1970s and 1980s by socialist feminists and Black feminism. Messner called these perspectives *multiple constructionism*, which were critical of the white, middle-class basis of feminist binary constructionism. Multiple constructionism argues that social categories should be seen as relationally constructed. The category woman, for example, must be understood in relation to the category man; the category homosexual must be understood in relation to the category heterosexual. Moreover, the boundaries between these categories are seen as ambiguous and fluid rather than hard and clear. Finally, as a reaction to the various forms of constructionism, Messner (2011) contends that a fourth perspective has emerged over the last couple of decades, which he calls *soft essentialism*. This perspective is currently ascendant. It seems to be much preferred by the professional class in society, that is, predominantly people in managerial positions. This perspective valorises 'individual choice' for girls and women, as if these choices are not conditional but entirely free. At the same time, however, soft essentialism retains a largely naturalised view of gender, meaning that gender is 'natural,' and that the genders are essentially different.

These various gender ideologies relate to different understandings of gender equity in the sense that certain gendered practices are understood as either natural and fair, or inherently unfair. For example, based on hard essentialism, it may well be the case that people feel that some sports are 'inappropriate' for one gender, because there is an essential difference between genders. Based on another perspective, where gender difference is seen as the result of social norms, assertions about 'naturalness' and generalisations regarding gender difference are interpreted as 'prejudiced.' There may well be gender differences, but why would that prevent women and men from participating in the same sports, for example (cf. Kempe-Bergman, 2014).

Returning to the notion of *gender performativity*, it resonates most with the third ideology, multiple constructionism. In this ideology, what gender means in each social situation or context is not taken for granted. Gender can be done – or performed – in many ways and it is not assumed that there are two genders. This view of gender can be linked to some other important concepts, which I will briefly define. Tightly linked to gender norms are sexuality norms, especially norms that assume people are heterosexual 'unless otherwise specified.' *Heteronormativity* is the name of this phenomenon. Heteronormativity can be seen as the driving force behind the idea that there are two 'opposite and complementary' genders (i.e., men are masculine, women are feminine). The alternatives to being heterosexual are homosexual (i.e., lesbian or gay) or bisexual, which means that you are attracted to people of the same gender, or of all genders.

Heteronormativity contributes to creating ideas about bodies, mainly that bodies are male or female and that people with male bodies identify as men while people with female bodies identify as women. *Cisgender (cis)*, which means 'on the same side,' designates persons who were assigned a certain gender at birth, and who grow up to identify as belonging to that same gender. *Transgender (trans)* designates that persons who were assigned one gender at birth, grow up to identify as belonging to another gender or to no specific gender. Hence, we talk about trans men, trans women, and non-binary people. *Intersex* designates people who, according to the Office of the United Nations High Commissioner for Human Rights "do not fit typical binary notions of male or female bodies" (HCHR, 2019). Intersex children are born in all societies, but in Western societies it is common for these children to be assigned one sex very early in life, which is not always the case in the developing world.

A key concept in the efforts to change gender power, at least if based in a gender performativity perspective, is *queer*. As an adjective, this term basically means 'strange' or 'odd.' As a noun, it is commonly understood as an umbrella term to encompass a range of gender identities and sexualities. However, it can also be seen as a verb: *to queer*. Viewing queer as a verb resonates with the perspective of gender performativity. Some people queer gender; that is, they do gender 'the wrong way,' in ways that break the norm. Queering gender can point in the direction of new and liberating ways of living and acting as human beings. In principle, actions associated with homosexuality and bisexuality, trans and intersex can be seen as different ways of queering dominant gender and heteronorms, but you do not have to be lesbian, gay, bisexual, trans, or intersex to queer, everyone can! Let me now introduce how issues of gender find expression in the context of movement cultures.

Movement Cultures: Sports and Physical Education

Movement is a prominent feature of humanity. People move in a multitude of ways and for a diversity of reasons. To some extent, humans move because we want to stay alive and produce the necessary things in life. In these cases, movements are underpinned by an instrumental rationale that means they can be scrutinised based on their function in relation to an intended outcome. Put simply, movements are judged based on if people stay alive and the quality and usefulness of the things that they produce. However, sometimes movements are judged for how they are experienced 'in themselves,' their intrinsic value. Such movements are about "the free process in which we express ourselves to reveal our uniqueness and distinctness" (Aggerholm, 2018, p. 200). In this way, movements also have existential value, they signal belongings and identities. Moreover, while some people prefer to participate in movements that include competition, others may prefer exercise without competition (Larsson & Larsson, 2021). A series of movement cultures have developed in which humans move simply because they like to move, for no other purpose than to move.

The notion of movement cultures has been theorised by Crum (1993) as how social groups deal with "the need and desire for movement beyond labor or maintaining life" (p. 341). Movement cultures consist of play, games, dance, acrobatic pursuits, etc., which people do for no other reasons than to move; it feels meaningful – or fun – to participate. Such practices, which can be found in virtually all historical and geographical contexts, are 'unnecessary' yet vital parts of human life. Although movement for movement's sake exists in most cultures, the values associated with the movements vary. Dance, for example, is perceived to be either a mainly masculine *or* feminine activity in different parts of the world. For example, while in the so-called Western world, dance is linked to femininity, in other parts of the world, such as in the Middle East, dance is linked to masculinity. At the same time, it must be emphasised that 'dance' is not the same in various parts of the world. Dancing can be many different things depending on time and place.

In modern societies, there is a strong trend in which movement cultures change from being spontaneously practiced, loosely organised, and non-institutionalised to becoming gradually more systematised, organised, and institutionalised for various purposes. Two contexts where movement cultures have been institutionalised are sports organisations and schools. Sports organisations concern clubs, associations, and federations at local, national, and international levels. Regarding schools, I am thinking foremost of physical education, which can be found in schools worldwide. In this book, I will pay particular attention to sports and physical education, and in chapter 2, I will present the historical background of these practices. Here, I want to point out that institutionalisation of movement cultures often means that the instrumentality and functionality of movements, which are included when movements have an extraneous purpose, are reinforced. Consequently, in sports and school physical education, instrumental values tend to be reinscribed in the movements – they become 'serious.' In sports, for example, movement skill learning among athletes is monitored and refined based on systematic considerations about performance enhancement, often backed by science. In school physical education, the movements of students may be monitored based on considerations about health, also backed by science. This means that in sports and physical education, what comes out of movements is examined and assessed based on how people achieve external goals ranging from winning competitions and setting records to living healthy lives. In these processes, the attitude towards the body, and the approach to movements may become more instrumental. The body is experienced as a tool or in need of control and discipline.

Most people have personal experience of sport and physical education, both positive and negative. To some extent, sport and physical education are overlapping phenomena, not least since sports comprise much of the content of contemporary physical education (Kirk, 1993). However, this does not mean that sport and physical education are interchangeable. For example, while competition is the purpose of sports, the purpose of physical education is education of the physical and through the physical (Arnold, 1979). The competition element inherent in sport, and sometimes also in physical education, probably also explains why the genders are often kept separate in these practices.

Gender and Sexuality in Sport and Physical Education

The world of sport is strongly affected by gender norms, which also mirrors that sports are to large extents characterised by segregation of the genders. In many ways, it seems reasonable to segregate the genders in sports, as gender segregation is typically considered to be a gender equity measure. In most sports contexts, it is perceived as unfair to compare the performances of women and men. However, in other parts of physical culture too, gender segregation also occurs, even if there is no direct comparison of the performances of women and men. This applies, for example, to recreational and exercise sports, including fitness gyms. Put simply, gender segregation appears appropriate because the genders are assumed to *be different*. But is it really as simple as that?

As gay, lesbian, bisexual, and intersex people have become increasingly visible and acknowledged in society over the past half century, it has become apparent that gender is more complex than one might at first think. Gender difference is, at most, *statistically* true albeit not necessarily true at an individual basis. This means that what is true for many, perhaps even for most, is not necessarily true for everyone and thus not for specific individuals. The gradual acceptance of other life forms than cis-gendered heterosexual ones has made clear that gender is not merely something that we 'are,' but also something that we 'do.' How we do gender is *not only* regulated by genes, hormones, or other biological factors, but also by a set of tacit agreements: *gender norms*. Norms are standards of proper or acceptable – or expected – behaviour. It is in relation to these standards of expected behaviour that people *do* gender – 'correctly' or 'incorrectly,' so to speak. To do gender incorrectly would be tantamount to queer gender, as described above (as a verb). In scientific literature, the notion of *doing gender*, which was coined in the mid-1980s by West and Zimmerman (1987), is frequently referred to as *gender performativity*, a term that was in turn outlined by Butler (1990) some years later. The notion of gender performativity is a key concept in this book and will be dealt with more extensively in chapter 3.

Sport is one social context where the notion of gender performativity is useful for critical analysis. Various sports are conditioned by factors that may well be attributed to biology, at least when it comes to performance levels, although later in the book I will illustrate how it can sometimes be the case that what we assume belongs to biology in fact may instead belong to culture. Or rather, what we assume is 'biology' is oftentimes the result of gender performativity. This means that what we assume exists 'from the beginning,' and which can explain behaviour, is rather the result of behaviour patterns that are regulated by social norms. This 'turn' opens completely new ways of understanding movement cultures and gender equity in these cultures.

Book Structure

The book is structured into seven chapters. This first chapter is followed by chapter 2, which concerns the origins of sports and physical education. Here, I highlight the purpose of sports and physical education when these social phenomena took their modern form – and who they were primarily intended for at the time. I will also discuss how interest in sports has broadened, while at the same time many of the original norms and values continue to dominate. What does this mean for today's participants in sport and physical education? How does it affect the opportunities to doing gender in these contexts?

Chapter 3 is devoted to the different theoretical perspectives that have developed parallel to the historical changes outlined in chapter 2. In essence, this involves what Hall (1988) labelled "from femininity to feminism" and the development of various theoretical strands within feminism. Particular attention is directed to the concept of gender performativity: what does it mean in the contexts of sports and physical education?

Chapter 4, 5, and 6 offer empirical examples of gender performativity taken from sports and physical education. Since the focus of the book is primarily on gender performativity as a tool to understand and change practice, rather than an overview of research, I will mainly, but not exclusively, use examples from my own research. With this follows that most examples are from a Swedish context. However, based on my reading of the literature, I can say that in essence, it differs only marginally from the situation in most Western countries. In the worlds of sport and physical education, there are nuances of gender that vary, but not the essence of what is perceived as gender. My ambition is to show how the notion of gender performativity can be used to understand critically and constructively – and potentially change:

- Gender in competitive sports (chapter 4),
- Gender in school physical education (chapter 5),
- LGBTQI+ issues (lesbian, gay, bisexual, trans, queer, intersex, and more) in sport (chapter 6).

Finally, in chapter 7, I will summarise the content of the previous chapters and devote some space to thinking about the future: how can the notion of gender performativity contribute to ongoing critical thinking about sports and physical education?

Questions

- Have you ever wondered about issues of gender equity in sports and physical education?

- If you have, why? If you have not, why?

- What if I ask the question like this: do you think that boys and girls, women and men, transgender people, intersex people, and non-binary people have the same opportunities to participate, enjoy and develop in sports and physical education?

- Do you think that bisexuals, homosexuals, heterosexuals, or people with all kinds of sexual orientations, all have the same opportunities to participate, enjoy and develop in sports and physical education?

CHAPTER 2

The Origins of Sports and Physical Education

Introduction

In this chapter, I describe the historical background of sports and physical education. Understanding this background is important to understand what gender means in these two contexts and how gender is currently performed. The view of gender has changed dramatically since sports and physical education emerged in their modern forms in the 1800s. All the various ideologies of gender that were presented in chapter 1 with reference to Messner (2011) – hard essentialism, binary constructionism, multiple constructionism, and soft essentialism – can be found also in sport and physical education.

In many ways, sport and physical education are 19th century inventions in Western countries that originally instilled a particular version of masculinity in boys and men. Gradually, however, they have come to attract people more broadly, but some of the original norms, for example, concerning masculinity and ability, remain relatively unchanged. Calls for gender equity relate to the possibilities for girls and women and other groups of people to participate in sport and physical education, and to do it in equal conditions compared with boys and men. These calls for gender equity have been followed by calls for inclusion of more previously marginalised groups, such LGBTQI+ people. Historically, this has meant that the view of gender has changed, but it has probably changed mostly on the surface and not so much in depth.

The Roots of Sports

Throughout history, evidence of sports-like practices can be found in a range of historical and geographical contexts. Ancient Greece, for example, is famous for its Olympic Games, which have been perceived as a model for modern Olympic Games. In Scandinavian countries, the word *idrott* (roughly 'sport') originated during the Viking Age from the Old Norse word *íþrótt* ('iː. θrouht) which designated strength, might, and valour (Loland, 2000). In the modern sense, however, sports originated in Britain in the 19th century. The institutional context for the development of modern sport, and particularly football (soccer), was the residence houses at public (independent) schools such as Winchester, Charterhouse, and Eton (Elias and Dunning, 1986). Here, sports grew to become a highly influential educational component.

There are some key aspects of modern sports that distinguish it from other sports-like cultural expressions. One such aspect is organisation and institutionalisation. It was typical that quite soon after the breakthrough at the British public schools, independent sports clubs, associations, and federations emerged. In this sense, sport became an independent phenomenon in civil society, which is also detectable in the conventional definition of sport: "physical contests pursued for the goals and challenges they entail" (Britannica.com/sports). Sport was attributed as an *intrinsic value*. However, this did not prevent it from being continuously associated also with various *instrumental values*, for example, character formation, education, health, and so on. At the same time, the view that sports had intrinsic value also meant that it came to be seen as non-political, non-ideological, and culturally neutral. This has had major consequences for sports, for example, in relation to gender equity.

Another aspect that distinguishes modern sports from most other sports-like phenomena is measurement and record keeping (e.g., world records). Accurate measuring made possible by technological progress that contributed to more accurate measuring instruments (such as the chronograph and later electric timing) meant an increasing quest for improvement. Previously, it had never been possible to compare results from separate competitions in separate places and on separate occasions. This quest for improvement has been compared with industrial society's emphasis on increased economic output and profit. Sports historian Thomas (1992) has shown how modern competitive sports spread from the British Isles to the European continent, North America, and eventually all parts of the world in the wake of industrialisation (see also Guttman, 2004).

A third aspect, which is crucial for this book and is sometimes overlooked in general descriptions of sports, is that modern sports originated in a decisively male context: the British public schools – for boys. This meant that practices that developed strength and character came to be associated with manliness. Olofsson (1989) has argued that "sport was created by men for men and have also been described by men" (through sports journalism and in sports research) (p. 11; author translation). However, girls and women have always showed an interest in sports, but historical records have tended to ignore that. For example, in ancient Greece, the Heraean Games for women existed parallel to the Olympic games. During the late 19th and early 20th centuries, women often took part alongside men in sporting events, especially in individual pursuits, such as running and skiing. Quite rapidly, however, they were banned from these events until around the 1970s and

80s, often under the pretext that a woman's constitution is not suitable for participation in 'male feats.'

Exclusion from male sports contexts urged women to create 'their own' sports practices. Thus, during the 1920s and 30s, special international federations for women's sports arranged the Women's World Games and the Women's Olympiad. As more women were gradually admitted into the men's federations and games, these special arrangements for women's sports faded away, for some to great despair. In the case of Sweden, The Swedish Women's Sports Federation was established in 1925, but it only lasted until 1929, when women's sports were included in the Swedish Sports Confederation.

Women and men have basically always been kept apart in sports competitions. It has been debated, however, whether the genders should do the same sports, in the same ways. In a lot of sports, minor 'adjustments' are made for women. For example, implements such as balls, throwing gear, net height and so on, are smaller/lighter/lower for women compared to men. One could of course say that men's equipment is bigger, heavier, or higher, but I have chosen the opposite wording because the rules of men's sport came first, and the rules of women's sport appeared later, in the form of 'adaptations' due to the gender constraints on women's participation at a certain point in time. Discussions about such adaptations are recurring, for example about the size of the football goal, or the height of the hurdles in athletics. It is unusual that the size of the goal in men's football is discussed, or the height of men's hurdles. This illustrates a hierarchical relationship, where women's sports are discussed and problematised in relation to men's sports, but not the opposite. Men's sports constitute the norm.

Occasionally, different sports for women have evolved, such as netball, softball, and ringette. These sports are 'adapted' versions of original male sports: basketball, baseball, and ice hockey. It is interesting to note, however, that these sports are mainly found in North America. The trend of creating 'female' versions of sports never really broke through in Europe. The dominating European trend has rather been to invite women to play the 'male' versions of sports. A recent example of a separatist sport is roller derby. While this sport has an older history in the US, it was revived in the early 2000s as a female, women-organised sport for women. As such, it has spread to many parts of the world and is profiled as a context that emphasises diversity.

Scrutinising the history of sport shows that certain human qualities prominent in sports are perceived as primarily masculine, or 'manly'. In short, sport was founded during the 1800s to promote autonomy, perseverance, and strength, i.e., traits that were considered masculine and highly valued in the formation of the British Empire. In contemporary societies, sport has gradually spread across nations and social groups and is now practiced by all kinds of people – but participation is still conditioned by the historical connection between sport and masculinity. Should these qualities be seen as 'natural' in men, but not in women? Or are they developed by and attributed to men due to social expectations for straight cis men to be and act in ways that are fit for purpose in sports? What would that mean for women, gay and bisexual men, and trans and intersex people?

The Roots of Physical Education

Physical education is the international designation of a school subject in primary and secondary education that exists in most countries in some form. There are many ways to justify the subject, but most justifications are based on the need for children and youth to be physically active for health purposes. Physical education is also taken to promote, for example, character, cooperation, and learning in other subjects (Bailey, et al., 2009). The intrinsic value of physical education is typically stated as "education through the physical" (Williams, 1930). According to Arnold (1979), physical education is about learning in, through, and about movement. The Swedish national curriculum states that physical education is about developing "all-round movement capabilities and interest in being physically active and spending time in nature" (SNAE, 2022, p. 48; author translation). To varying degrees in different parts of the world, teaching in the subject is based on sports, play, dance, fitness activities, and outdoor activities.

A few decades ago, there was strong international rhetoric stating that the subject was in crisis (Griffey, 1987; Kirk, 1996; Tinning and Fitzclarence, 1992). Some held that the subject had an increasingly marginalised position in the education system in most countries (Marshal and Hardman, 2000). However, at least in some countries, it seems that the subject has recovered somewhat during the past two decades. In Sweden, for example, the total number of hours devoted to the subject increased in 2020 from 500 to 600 throughout the nine-years of compulsory schooling, the result of a government decision. Arguably, the recovery is due to the increased social anxiety around sedentary behaviour among children and youth, which is perceived to be detrimental to their health. A special issue of the reputable scientific journal *The Lancet* even talked about a 'physical inactivity pandemic' (Kohl, et al., 2012). Currently, it seems that physical education has a secure place in the school curriculum.

In Sweden and many other countries, co-education is standard in physical education. This seems to be in perfect order, at least if the teaching does not include too much competition. If it does, concerned voices are often raised, stating that there should be separate teaching for girls and boys. On such occasions behaviours appear to be excused based on the reasoning 'that's just the way boys/girls are,' and that girls and boys should therefore be kept separate to 'protect' each other. For example, boys are sometimes perceived as boisterous to the extent that girls should be protected from them. Conversely, girls are sometimes perceived to be weak and non-athletic to the extent that boys should not be dragged with girls during physical education lessons.

Physical education was a key element in the emergence of modern education systems during the 19th century. Sweden is an illustrative example for a development that was similar in many countries. A national curriculum for the state grammar schools, which included physical education, was enforced by law in 1820. Grammar schools were academically oriented schools dedicated to the children of society's elite. Until 1927, however, girls were not allowed to enter grammar schools. They could graduate as private students or at special private girls' schools, in which the conditions for physical education were poor. Elementary schools became mandatory for all children in 1842 and physical education became a mandatory subject from the start. Teaching was co-educational up until the early decades of the 20th century. This is likely due to the dominance of educational gymnastics, also known as Swedish gymnastics, which did not include any competitive elements.

Swedish gymnastics was developed by Per Henrik Ling (1776-1839) at The Royal Central Gymnastics Institute (founded in 1813) in Stockholm. This sort of gymnastics, which should not be confused with modern artistic gymnastics, was practiced in large groups who in unison performed structured movements led by a gymnastics director. Of today's forms of gymnastics, troupe gymnastics, at least the floor exercise, is reminiscent of Swedish gymnastics, which, however, did not contain any acrobatic and competitive elements. Ling's basic idea was that the body should be educated in a balanced way, with a focus on harmonic movements, without any form of competition and specialisation of movements and body parts (Ljunggren, 2000).

Ling's ambition to create a comprehensive gymnastics system was shared by his son, Hjalmar Ling (1820-1886), who focused on educational gymnastics. While Per Henrik Ling's idea of gymnastics rested on an organic perspective where the body was viewed as a temple of the soul, Hjalmar Ling's gymnastics system framed the body more as a machine which was to be disciplined and 'well-oiled' (Ljunggren, 2000). This development meant that Swedish gymnastics evolved into becoming a rather rigid exercise, which was not very popular among students. There were attempts to modernise the practice, including gymnastics pedagogue Elin Falk's efforts to reform children's gymnastics in the early 1900s, but by the middle of the 20th century, gymnastics was no longer perceived as compatible with the goals set for physical education (Lundquist Wanneberg, 2004; see also Kirk, 1992). Instead, other movement activities were implemented, such as play, dance, outdoor pursuits – and sports.

The introduction of sports into physical education curricula, which commenced early in the 20th century, also meant an incentive to separate girls and boys. Separate curricula for boys and girls were established at a national level. While competition and strenuous physical activity was considered more appropriate for boys, graceful and 'aesthetic' movements were considered more appropriate for girls, although the two curricula certainly overlapped. At this time, traits like these were considered to mirror the natures of boys and girls. This reflects a hard essentialist view of gender (Messner, 2011), which means the perception that there are characteristics that separate the sexes and that cannot be affected. This situation lasted well into modern times. It was not until a school reform in 1980 that the gender differentiated physical education curriculum was abandoned and co-education was mandated in Swedish schools. The introduction of co-education was clearly a gender equity measure based not on essentialism, but on constructionism (Messner, 2011), that is, the view that gender differences are mainly rooted in different social and cultural norms. The basic idea was that the school should not reinforce gender norms that otherwise dominate in society but challenge them. However, as I will illustrate in a later chapter because gender norms in the subject had solidified, concerns about gender inequities arose because of the introduction of co-education, rather than the opposite (Carli, 2004). I contend that in such a situation, rather than falling back into essentialist assumptions about gender, the notion of gender performativity is particularly useful to think critically about gender equity.

Gender Equity in Sports

In the previous sections, I presented the historical development of sports and physical education. I emphasised their masculine background, but also pointed to the trend that over time, people of all kinds have started to play sports and participate in physical education. Still, the dominance of masculinity is clear, which opens for discussions about *gender equity*. Typically, gender equity, equal opportunity, or equality of opportunity, designates "the idea that people ought to be able to compete on equal terms, or on a 'level playing field,' for advantaged offices and positions" (Britannica.com/equal-opportunity). In sports, the critical question becomes what 'compete on equal terms' means. In the encyclopaedia, one can assume that 'compete on equal terms for advantaged offices and positions' means potentially *the same* advantaged offices and positions, regardless of gender. In sports, however, gender equity is typically about the ability for women and men to participate on equal terms, and to have equal access to resources for participation, *in two separate arenas*. Due to the historical background of sport, which was strongly linked to male character formation, definitions of gender equity often focus specifically on dismantling the perception that sport is a 'male' venture and that men are better suited to pursue sports, such as in the policy of the European Institute for Gender Equality (EIGE):

> Gender equality in sport means breaking down the harmful stereotypes that continue to make women less likely to take up sporting activities. It also means promoting women's advancement as professional athletes and leaders in the sport sector. (EIGE/sports)

While most people would agree that gender equity is desirable, it is contested when equitable opportunities and obligations exist in practice and what measures are necessary to reach an equitable situation. To some extent, as was discussed in chapter one, people with different views of gender may also have different views of gender equity.

The choice to stick to gender segregation in sports is likely because the physical prerequisites for participation are perceived by many to be so different between the genders that segregation still appears the best arrangement. By extension, this means that women and men must have the same conditions – the same rights and obligations – to participate in their own sports arenas. In a European context, gender equity means that all sports must be open for both male and female participation, and that resources must be allocated on equal terms to female and male athletes within each and the same sport. Overall, this is also true in North

America, but there resources must be allocated on equal terms to women's and men's sports, but not *necessarily* to the same sports.

In US, gender equity legislation, or the Title IX,[1] has been negotiated in particular ways to fit the context of American scholastic sports, that is, sports in high schools and universities. The key part of Title IX, signed into law in 1972, reads:

> No person in the United States shall, based on sex, be excluded from participation in, be denied the benefits of, or be subjected to discrimination under any education program or activity receiving Federal financial assistance. (Title IX, Education Amendments Act of 1972, 2018).

The law means that American universities can either create measures against skewed participation among women and men in one and the same sport, or they can offer participation in different sports for women and men. The main thing is that overall participation and resource allocation is proportional.

After many years of work with gender equity, and because of a strong focus on the contemporary rhetoric of individual freedom, there is now a tendency for people to believe that equity has already been achieved. This became apparent in a Swedish study by Kempe-Bergman and colleagues (2020), who conducted in-depth interviews with 60 male youth sport leaders and coaches. These interviews also shed light on the fact that the meaning of gender equity covaries with different meanings of 'gender.' Kempe-Bergman identified four different attitudes among the male sports leaders and coaches, 'the sceptic,' 'the cynic,' 'the women's rights activist,' and 'the constructionist,' which are described in the following sections.

While the sceptic and the cynic were negative about the need

---

[1] 'Title IX' refers to a federal civil rights law in the United States that was enacted as part (Title IX) of the Education Amendments of 1972.

for gender equity efforts, the women's rights activist and the constructionist were positive. Three of the attitudes, the sceptic, the cynic, and the women's rights activist articulated an understanding about gender that can be labelled soft essentialism (Messner, 2011), which means that people valorise "the liberal feminist ideal of individual choice for girls and women, while retaining a largely naturalised view of boys and men" (p. 155). In more everyday terms, this means a perception that the genders are different and that gender patterns are unproblematic because girls and women, boys and men are free to choose as they wish. The constructionist, on the other hand, called for a need for more gender equity efforts because traditional gender norms still prevail and limit possibilities for participation for both girls (in traditional 'boy sports,' such as ice hockey) and boys (in traditional 'girl sports,' such as gymnastics). This attitude resonates with what Messner (2011) calls multiple constructionism.

The sceptic and the cynic were both altogether negative about the need for gender equity efforts, but they were negative for varied reasons. The sceptic was sceptical because he considered that there is no longer any inequality. Girls and boys, men and women are free to do whatever they want, and existing skewed gender patterns are not the result of stereotypes or anything else that hinders participation. Skewed gender patterns are rather understood as coming from 'natural' gender differences. The cynic held that 'full equality will never occur' – because the genders are 'naturally' different. Consequently, this attitude was linked to an understanding of gender equity as an attempt to eradicate gender difference (Kempe Bergman, et al., 2020).

Sport is indeed a challenging context for gender equity, both because of sport's history of male domination and strong links to masculinity, and because it is still considered legitimate to separate the genders, at least in competitive situations. Women and men are then entitled to the same rights and obligations, but in two separate arenas.

Gender Equity in Physical Education

Reasoning about gender equity in physical education is both similar to and different from gender equity in sports. When gymnastics dominated the curriculum, girls and boys were taught together, but were separated when sports gained more prominence in the curriculum. However, it did not mean that physical education was automatically co-educational, as girls were often barred from entering public secondary education. Co-educational gymnastics/physical education occurred in primary schools only. In Sweden, teenage girls were allowed into the state-run secondary schools in 1927. By that time, sport and other movement activities, such as play, dance, and outdoor activities were prominent in the curriculum. Moreover, around the turn of the 20th century, gymnastics was differentiated into 'male' and 'female' versions, where the male version emphasised strength and fitness to a larger extent, while the female version emphasised mobility and grace. So, while girls and boys were taught most subjects in gender-mixed classes, physical education remained for a long time the only segregated subject. The segregation was more expedient as more (competitive) sports came to dominate the physical education curriculum.

In 1962, a large school reform was implemented in Sweden and physical education (then still called Gymnastics) was included in both primary and secondary schools. This curriculum focused on recreational, yet 'economic,' 'aesthetic,' and controlled movements, and an overall versatile and harmonious development (SNSB, 1962). Ideas about team spirit, self-discipline, helpfulness, and leadership also played a prominent role. Regarding gender, the following regulations applied: "From year 5 onwards, girls and boys shall, if possible, form separate groups" (SNSB, 1962, p. 344). For girls, gymnastics and dance were emphasised, and for boys, sport skills and fitness. There were no reasons given as to why girls and boys should be taught separately, nor why the content should be different. In 1969, the gendered differentiation was removed, but nothing was said about the preferred teaching form. In practice, gender separate physical education classes remained (Lundquist Wanneberg, 2004). The concept of 'gender equity' appeared for the first time in the general national curriculum, which now stated that "the school should work for gender equity" (SNSB, 1969, p. 14; author translation). Moreover, it was stated that "boys and girls shall receive the same education and be stimulated to be interested in the same kind of work tasks in different subjects" as well as that "the school shall direct the same social expectations towards both genders" (p. 5).

Then in 1980, physical education was re-named from Gymnastics to Sport, the final scrapping of (Swedish) gymnastics. The national curriculum now focused on "regular physical activity as a means of health and well-being" and students' physical, mental, and social development (SNSB 1980, p. 90). While the name of the subject signalled an increased focus on sports, the content had an increased focus on health. In the following year, school authorities issued a complementing directive stipulating that co-education was to be the standard teaching method. Co-education was seen as "a means of equalising gender roles" as it "can be part of the school's task to work for equality between women and men" (SNSB 1981, p. 110). This can be interpreted as a turn in a clear constructionist direction (cf., Messner, 2011).

Co-education did not, however, have the expected results and many felt that the situation for girls worsened. Co-education did not change the traditional view of gender. The many years of gender-differentiated teaching had naturalised the connections between girls and aesthetic movements and dance, and boys and sports skills and fitness. Many teachers felt that rather than increasing gender equity, co-education meant that girls had to give way to athletic boys. Few noted, however, that the content previously linked specifically to boys' physical education now came to dominate the overall curriculum, at the expense of other content linked to girls' physical education. Dance was marginalised, practiced – if at all – in a few lessons each semester. Games, which had previously dominated boys' physical education, became mainstream co-educational content. In this situation, some teachers started to lament the abandonment of gender separate teaching (Carli, 2004).

In 1994, the current wording regarding gender equity was included: "The school has a responsibility to counteract traditional gender patterns. It should therefore allow students to test and develop their abilities and interests regardless of gender" (SNAE, 1994, p. 6). This is a requirement for teachers to act more actively to promote gender equity. The national physical education curriculum also stated that "The teaching must take into account the students' different conditions and contribute to gender equity by taking into account the gender differences that exist between girls and boys when it comes to, e.g., physical ability, risk of injury, body image and other conditions" (SNAE, 1994, p. 30). The formulation was found to be contradictory and was omitted by the SNAE (Swedish National Agency of Education) in the year 2000.

The last 50-60 years have seen a radical shift from gender-segregated teaching based on essentialist notions of 'natural' gender, to gender-integrated (co-educational) teaching based on constructionist notions of gender that challenge gender norms. This development is similar in most Western countries. Nevertheless, while constructionist ideas serve as the basis of curriculum document, physical education practice seems still to be dominated by essentialist ideologies of gender.

Conclusion

This chapter outlined the development of sports and physical education. Both contexts are permeated by what are conventionally seen as masculine values, but are they masculine because men and boys have dominated the practice (an essentialist understanding), or because they instil masculine qualities in men and boys (a binary constructionist understanding)? Paradoxically, while both practices were considered to instil 'manly' traits in men, they were at the same time considered to be 'natural' to men from the very beginning. In the case of modern sports, its growth was, at least to some extent, rooted in the British Empire's need for leaders to administer colonial rule. Therefore, competitive instinct and individual initiative became prominent in this culture. In the case of physical education, where Swedish gymnastics was particularly prominent, the needs were rooted in military needs. Therefore, collectively ordered discipline and character were prioritized.

Despite both practices emphasising masculine values, women and girls began to participate alongside the men and boys. For a period, women's participation was allowed, but only within their own defined sphere of sport and physical education. Women and men were strictly held apart and this segregation became a cornerstone in reasoning about equity. 'Equal conditions' initially meant the right to participate in activities that were adapted to the characteristics seen as inherent in each gender. Gradually, the meaning shifted to become a right to participate in activities that were basically identical, but where the genders were separated.

This meaning of gender equity is still dominant in sports. In physical education, however, gender equity has now come to mean that girls and boys should have opportunities to participate in a common educational activity. These different perceptions of how the relationship between girls and boys, men and women should be organised place different demands on how to think about gender equity. Moreover, the issue of gender equity is particularly challenging in relation to LGTBI+ issues.

The content of this book is based on the idea that the notion of gender performativity is particularly relevant to thinking critically about gender equity in sports and physical education, where gender norms are perceived as the major barrier. In the next chapter I will therefore pay special attention to this concept, its emergence and meaning.

Questions

- What are your experiences of participation in sports and physical education?
- Do you feel that the activities you have participated in have been fair? What does 'fair' mean then?
- If not, what have you experienced as unfair? How could that change?
- Can experiences of injustice be related to your gender identification or sexual orientation?

CHAPTER 3

Theorising Gender. Outlining Gender Performativity

Introduction

This chapter will focus on different theoretical perspectives that developed in parallel to the historical changes in sports and physical education outlined in the previous chapter. In essence, this development involves what Hall (1988) called 'from femininity to feminism.' A century ago, few protested against women and men being kept apart and engaging in separate tasks; today it is more common to challenge such stereotypical perceptions. Feminism is the approach that aims to achieve gender equity and counter gender norms and their consequences. In academia, feminism aims to illuminate gender-based injustice and contribute to increased equity. However, academic feminism is not a unified tradition of thought. I will start the chapter with mapping the most influential feminist strands. Particular attention will then be directed to an ascendant feminism, where the concept of performativity holds a central position. Knowledge about various feminist strands is important to develop different understandings of gender patterns in sport and physical education and to understand different approaches to gender equity.

Gender, Sex – What is It?

Sports and physical education are permeated almost completely by gender. For example, boys and girls, women and men use separate changing rooms, and, in many cases, they change into training clothes that differ in design. Moreover, in numerous sports practices, men and women are separated, either because there are rules that stipulate this separation, or because it is what a lot of people prefer for various reasons. However, this separation is probably something few pay much attention to. 'That's just the way it is.' Or at least, the practice is experienced as unproblematic if you meet current expectations of what it means to be male or female. But before I start problematising gender segregation, I will briefly relate to the conventional rationale behind this practice.

Gender segregation is typically considered to be appropriate because the genders are different. So far, I have used the word *gender* as a collective word for women and men, male and female, but possibly, I should really have used the word *sex*. How so? While gender typically refers to socially constructed characteristics of women, men, girls and boys, sex as a noun refers to biological characteristics, most often ones that are related to reproduction, and sex as a verb refers to reproductive activities. As such, sex seems often to be perceived as more 'real' than gender because 'social constructs' can be perceived as objectively 'unreal.' This is a position that I do not advocate, but which seems to dominate the public consciousness. But what does all this have to do with sports and physical education? The use of separate changing rooms, for example, is probably by many assumed to be rooted in 'natural' characteristics that have to do with biological sex. At the same time, the practice can also be explained by factors rooted in historical ideas of acceptability and prudishness, notions that I mean are rather covered by the concept of gender. Separate changing rooms may be used with reference to sex, but the use of separate changing rooms can also be seen as producing and reproducing the idea of sex.

The sexes are also separated in sports. It is difficult to ignore that certain statistical differences exist between women and men that are attributed significance in connection with sports competitions. Among other things, these differences are about physical differences, such as that men are *statistically* larger (taller, heavier) and can develop greater physical power. In terms of sports, the statistical differences have meant that sports organisations have found it appropriate to create two different competition classes.

So far, this account is based on the notion that sex, a reproductive function among human beings, gains wide significance in life more broadly. Reproductive or biological functions have far-reaching consequences for activities that are not directly related to reproduction. For example, linking certain characteristics and abilities to either sex means that the sexes need to be separated in sport competitions. Possibly, everything would have been peace and joy if these observations that justify gender segregation had been all-encompassing, but that is not the case (e.g., not all men are larger or stronger than all women). While the reproductive function may be absolute (i.e., it takes two different germ cells to conceive a child), secondary gender characteristics and differences are statistical in nature. The overlaps between the sexes are large. When looking at individuals, there are more similarities between women and men as there are differences. Moreover, also the assumption that all men and women are sexually attracted to the 'opposite sex' falls short. In other words, something further is needed to explain the many 'sex differences' that societies exhibit. In this way, a conceptual division between biological and environmental inheritance has arisen, that is, a division between sex and gender.

While 'biological inheritance' suggests that some sex characteristics are innate or 'natural,' 'environmental inheritance' suggests that other sex characteristics are learned or 'acquired.' The word *gender* designates qualities assumed to be learned or in some way acquired. However, sex and gender are often used interchangeably or synonymously. Historically, what has been considered natural (sex) or acquired (gender) has greatly varied. The so-called 'nature nurture debate' is still ongoing, even if the scientific conversation is now increasingly characterized by various attempts to see beyond the opposite relationship (e.g., Barlow, 2019). It revolves around the relative contributions to human development of 1) genetic inheritance and 2) environmental factors. This debate is based on the notion that human behaviour is the net outcome of genetic inheritance and environmental factors, but that the impact of either side may vary. For example, it is unclear to what extent genetic inheritance or environmental factors can explain gender differences regarding endurance, strength, and even game-sense. Also, the existence of homosexuality has been discussed based on assumptions about genetics or environment (e.g., Jannini, et al., 2010). It should be noted, though, that this discussion concerns why homosexuality exists, as if it must be explained, while heterosexuality apparently needs no such explanation.

In principle, however, the assumption that certain gender characteristics are acquired is not hugely different from the assumption that they are caused by genes. In either case, there is something – 'nature', 'genetics', 'culture', or 'environment' – that is *behind*, and can explain, sex/gender. Sex/gender separation is typically seen as a logical arrangement based on a difference that is taken to exist within humans, whether this difference is genetically inherited or environmentally acquired. In sport competitions, anthropometric and physiological differences between the sexes/genders justify the two competition classes, regardless of great individual variation and quite substantial overlap between the categories.

It is worth noticing that biological reasoning is sometimes associated with conservative views of gender (sex differences are natural and sports activities must be 'adapted' based on these'), as was the case with 'the sceptic,' and 'the cynic' viewpoint discussed in the previous chapter. Environmental reasoning tends to be associated with progressive views (gender differences are learned and can therefore be re-learned or changed), as was the case with 'the constructionist' viewpoint (Kempe-Bergman, et al., 2020). However, this is a generalisation. In the remainder of the chapter, I will mainly focus on progressive viewpoints: *feminist* perspectives that aim to change the norm.

From Femininity to Feminism in Sport

Writing in 1988, influential sport sociologist M. Ann Hall asserted "that there are unrecognised gender assumptions and ideologies implicit in sport research" (Hall, 1988, p. 331). According to Hall, sport research carried a set of assumptions that researchers needed to come to terms with to avoid oppressing female and non-heterosexual athletes. One such assumption was that talking and researching about 'gender' in fact meant research on *women*. A focus on women was both positive and negative. On the positive side, women had been previously overlooked in research to a considerable extent. Most research was conducted on male athletes by male researchers. Researching women in sport thus meant a welcome addition to sports research.

On the negative side, a lot of the gender/women sport research was implicitly about what female athletes were *lacking* or how they *differed* in relation to male athletes. Critical interlocutors noted that research often started from the sometimes-implicit question 'how are women different from men?' The reverse question, 'how are men different from women?' was rarely, if ever, evoked (Birrell, 1984). In research, this mainly contributed to the assumption that men participate in sports, whereas women participate in *women's* sports. While this probably helped maintain the privileged position men's sport was attributed, arguably, it also contributed to obscure the view that certain sports experiences could be potentially harmful to men as well as women.

Hall (1988) demonstrated how the early research on sportswomen sometimes revolved around issues rooted in the fear that they would become manly and lose their femininity, which included 'their heterosexual attraction' or their heterosexuality altogether. Paradoxically, while gender separation is typically justified based on the notion that gender differences are 'natural' (i.e., innate) and as such non-changeable, the fear that women could somehow become manly, even lesbian, through participation in strenuous and competitive sports supported the notion that gender differences result from environmental factors. At the heart of Hall's (1988) critique of sports research up to the 1980s was a questioning of the concept of 'sex/gender role,' widely used at the time. The following quote illustrates Hall's positioning:

> It (i.e., sex role) is illogical because we do not attempt to explain differential behavior patterns on the basis of race, age, or social class alone, but we do explain them in terms of a power differential that certainly coincides with race, class, and age distinctions. The notion of role focuses attention more on individuals than on social structure and depoliticizes the central questions of power and control in explaining gender inequality. (Hall, 1988, p. 334)

Hall (1988) drew on the assertion that sex roles resemble a "boxcar carrying an assortment of sociological and psychological data along with an explosive mixture of myth and untested assumptions" (Sherif, 1982, p. 392, cited in Hall, 1988, p. 334). This illustrates why a critical perspective, that is, *a power perspective*, is needed in research on gender in sports. Enter: feminism!

Waves and Strands of Feminism.

Critical approaches to gender inequities are sometimes depicted as 'waves' of feminism, which may or may not be connected to various academic 'strands' of feminism (Lewis, Benschop and Simpson, 2018). The first wave occurred in Western countries during the 19th and early 20th centuries and is linked to women's suffrage, political influence, and opportunities to control their own lives. The second wave occurred in the decades following World War II and continued until the 1970s. It maintained that while women had been given the right to vote, formal political influence, and opportunities to control their own lives, unlike men, they were still circumscribed by ideas and ideals that prevented them from exerting their rights. The third wave occurred during the 1990s. Among other things, it dwelled on the possibilities for people to lead their lives as individuals, rather than genders. This approach paved the way for a fourth wave of feminism, which in recent decades has meant an increased focus on the *intersections* between gender and other potentially stigmatising and limiting categorisations, such as class, race, sexuality, trans, and so on.

However, Lewis and colleagues (2018) point out that the wave metaphor "suggests a temporality with one distinct wave after the other, but it is more helpful to see the feminist waves as particular approaches than to pin them to distinct periods in time" (p. 4). To some extent, the waves exist simultaneously. This means that the umbrella concept feminism has come to denote various and sometimes contradictory ambitions and approaches. What they have in common, though, is an aspiration to combat gender stereotypes and change gender-related injustice.

To complicate the issue further, I will now return to the various academic 'strands' of feminism mentioned by Lewis and colleagues (2018). For pedagogical reasons, I will here limit my account to three feminist strands: liberal, socialist, and radical.

Liberal feminism is loosely linked to the first wave of feminism. Its basic ideas are often accredited to liberal philosopher John Stuart Mill (1806-1873) and his book *The Subjection of Woman* (Mill, 1869). However, Mary Wollstonecraft (1759-1797) had presented similar ideas in her book *A Vindication of the Rights of Woman* in the late 1700s (Wollstonecraft, 2004/1792). According to liberal feminism, the prevailing power order is based on women's exclusion from public space, both politically and professionally. Women's alleged weakness is not rooted primarily in nature, but rather in upbringing and (lack of) education. The situation described by Wollstonecraft and Mill is still valid in parts of the world, which makes the ideas of liberal feminism still relevant.

Socialist feminism is inspired by the writings of Karl Marx (1818-1883), and perhaps to an even greater extent his associate Friedrich Engels (1820-1895) who authored the book *The Origin of the Family, Private Property and the State* (1909/1884). According to socialist feminism, gender inequality is linked to the dominate system of production and accumulation of capital in modern society: capitalism. Moreover, capitalism is linked to patriarchy, an institutionalised social system in which some men (the bourgeoisie) dominate over others, including women. Socialist feminists have offered vivid examples of how, in the quest to get out of one system (patriarchy and submission to male relatives), women end up in the trap of the other system: capitalism and underpaid labour in the public sector. One example of this is the entry of women into the labour market. To free themselves from economic dependence on their male relatives, many women have ended up in low-paid jobs within the public sector, for example, in care and education.

Radical feminism, the third scholarly feminist strand, traces its ideas to Shulamith Firestone's (1945-2012) *The Dialectic of Sex: A Case for Feminist Revolution* (2003/1970) and Kate Millett's (1934-2017) *Sexual Politics* (2000/1970). The notion of patriarchy is key in radical feminism, but while socialist feminism identifies capitalism as the most basic system of power, radical feminists see patriarchy as the most basic system of power. Patriarchy designates the norms that regulate relationships between women and men, including women's and men's roles in connection with reproduction, child rearing, family life, income, and so on. Within patriarchy, men's exercise of power over women is based on threats of violence – which are sometimes realised. Sexual harassment, sexual abuse, and rape are integral to the exercise of power and attempts to control women's (sexual) freedom.

These various waves and strands of feminism have had huge social, political, and scholarly impacts. However, they are all based on the premise that there 'are' genders. Specifically, that there are *two* genders that are rather homogeneous and constitute mutually exclusive categories. During the 1990s, scholarly thinking that strongly challenged this perspective made its breakthrough. Rather than what gender 'is,' this perspective highlights how people *do* gender in various social contexts. It is the doing of gender that produces the belief that there 'are' two sexes. Such a perspective allows thinking outside of the gender-binary. Additionally, because of a more process-oriented approach, it may convey better possibilities for scholarly work to bring about change. I will now devote the remainder of the chapter to this perspective.

Gender Performativity

The notion of performativity signals a paradigm shift – a shift in the basic way of thinking about and relating to reality. Performativity shifts the focus from substance ('what *is*') to process ('what *does*'). This shift is illustrated by a change in researchers' language from nouns, typically in singular, such as '*the* woman', '*the* man', '*the* body', *et cetera*, to verbs, such as doing, performing, enacting, materialising, embodying, *et cetera*. In fact, verbs based on the above nouns are sometimes created in research, such as 'gendering' and 'bodying' (e.g., Anderson, 2003; Hovden, 2010; Theberge, 2006). The paradigm shift has also meant changes in how researchers do research. Research that includes various types of measurements that are used for statistical (or *quantitative*) analysis, for example regarding bodily functions or participant patterns in different sports, must necessarily start from an assumption that the category exists before the measurement and that individuals within the category share at least some characteristics that make it justifiable to talk about a category of people. Such research is still important and can bring new light on power structures and changes to them over time and across cultures, for example. This type of research has been supplemented by other research that includes what is typically called *qualitative* analysis. Here, focus is primarily on processes. For example, through exploring the processes of various sociocultural contexts researchers can offer clues about what constitutes categories such as gender (i.e., cis, trans, intersex) and how these categories relate to participation patterns in different sports. I will now trace the background to this process-oriented perspective.

Performance or Performativity?

Until now, I have used the concept of performativity as a synonym for the expression 'doing gender.' Sometimes performativity is also mixed up with the concept of performance. Therefore, I will disentangle these concepts here. To start with the notion of *doing gender*, it was coined by American sociologists Candace West and Don Zimmerman in 1987. Overall, West and Zimmermann's (1987) endeavour was "to advance a new understanding of gender as a routine accomplishment embedded in everyday interaction" (p. 125). Theoretical inspiration for this endeavour was taken from anthropology, particularly from Erving Goffman's notion of *performance* as theorised in "Gender Display" (Goffman, 1976). In this book, Goffman highlighted that people 'read' each other based on their respective performances, the actions performed by individuals that make them recognisable as belonging to a certain category of people. West and Zimmermann (1987) asserted that practically all social situations include 'markers' that signify gender and that we as humans are very skilled in the practice of decoding gender, partly because most people are also skilled performers as women or men in leisurely and practically 'unconscious' ways.

Concerning movements, Young (1980) and Connell (1983) provided early illustrations of doing gender. Young (1980), for example, noted that many girls restrict their spatial outreach as they 'throw like a girl.' Connell (1983) highlighted that many boys, conversely, frequently invade space in their noisy and boisterous physical play. Such actions, conventionally explained by 'that's how girls and boys *are*,' are responses by individuals and groups of individuals to *gender norms* – standards of acceptable behaviour for girls and boys, women, and men.

Like most thought-provoking theory, the notion of doing gender has also met critique. Despite focusing on doing, or how practice produces categories of people (genders), in West and Zimmermann's account genders still exist *a priori* in the sense that it is women and men who perform the actions that make them intelligible (or not) as women or men. Performances are performed by performers, almost as in the case of acting. This highlights that performance and performativity, despite the linguistic similarity, signify different paradigms. As Brickell (2003, p. 158) notes, "[d]espite the popularity of performativity and performance as metaphors for exploring gender, the two terms are themselves often confused and their theoretical first principles elided. This confusion arises in part because performance and performativity have quite different antecedents, even though the terms themselves are often regarded as synonymous." For the remainder of this chapter, I will focus entirely on the notion of *performativity* and explore its theoretical foundations.

Speech Act Theory

Judith Butler's books *Gender Trouble* (Butler, 1990) and *Bodies That Matter* (Butler, 1993) spearheaded the notion of *gender performativity* in feminist research. While one of Butler's later books, *Undoing Gender* (Butler, 2004), seems an allusion to West and Zimmermann's 1987-piece, Butler did not refer to their work (although she does refer to Goffman's work). Instead, Butler found inspiration in linguistics and particularly in *speech act theory* (Austin, 1962). This theory was originally formulated in the mid-20th century by Cavanaugh (2015, p. 1), who eloquently described it as designating "the power of language to effect change in the world." Speech act theory holds that language is not only a way of passively describing the world, "but may instead (or also) function as a form of social action" (Cavanaugh, 2015, p. 1).

This way of thinking began in relation to speech acts that produce obvious social changes, such as when priests utter 'I pronounce you husband and wife' and 'I baptise you.' The action is founded in a social *naming* of a practice that evokes a new or changed reality. Austin (1962) called this function of language *performative utterances*, or *performatives* (notably, rather than performances).

The notion that language can have a performative function, that it can effect change in the world through naming, has wide significance. In situations where language is thought to be passively describing a state of affairs, it is possible to see how the naming brings the state of affairs into existence. For example, when a child is born, the first thing said is rarely 'it's a child!' but rather 'it's a boy!' or 'it's a girl!' This signifies that what is important is not whether the child is a child, but what gender the child is. It is assumed that the child is a child, but the gender of the child is open. Though at first glance it may be assumed that the child can be *either* a *girl or* a boy (and nothing else), this may well be jumping to a conclusion.

Poststructuralist Performativity.

Before moving on to Butler's conceptualisation of the concept of performativity, a few words must be said about poststructuralism. Poststructuralism is a school of thought emanating from continental European, specifically French, philosophy in the 1960s and 70s. It is based on the idea that the meaning of a word or a phrase is not primarily established by its relationship to a 'real' object, but by its relationship to objects *and* other words and phrases. Meaning in language is built in and through a *structure* of relationships, hence structuralism. While scholars of the preceding period, during the mid-1900s, were mainly occupied by the structures themselves, and *the* language (the whole), poststructuralist thinkers such as Michel Foucault were more interested in exploring how language structures were used – and changed – in and through practice in local contexts, hence *post*-structuralism. Moreover, while language had a somewhat narrower meaning within structuralism, chiefly limited to what we usually mean by 'language,' within poststructuralism, the meaning of language was broadened to include all sorts of practices that contribute to the creation of meaning. Such an approach allows for analyses of how 'male' and 'female' are *practiced* (or done), not only talked about, in local contexts. Researchers can explore what gender means in various contexts without necessarily having to relate to what gender 'really' is.

While it is often assumed that from a biological perspective there are two genders, some biologists, such as Fausto-Sterling (2000), assert that there are in fact more genders, or that gender is a potentiality rather than a facticity. In social life, however, it is conventionally taken for granted that there 'are' two genders: male and female. Butler holds that this limitation of the number of genders relates to what she calls a *heterosexual matrix*. The heterosexual matrix is a perceptual grid through which humans, their looks, actions, and their whole being are interpreted (Butler 1990, Chapter 2). In effect, while biology allows for a diversity of genders, contemporary societies rarely allow for more than two – and this is regulated and manifested in the utterances like 'it's a boy!' or 'it's a girl!' As I mentioned before, naming the gender of a baby is not a passive description of something obvious, it marks the beginning of a whole practice that will characterise interactions between the child and people in its environment. In most cases, this practice will assume that the baby grows up to become a heterosexual girl or boy. This is *heteronormativity*, the implicit assumption that people are heterosexual. Thus, the heterosexual matrix contributes to perform the (two) genders taken for granted as already existing from the beginning.

Not only does heteronormativity assume people are heterosexual, but it also means that the genders are taken to be 'natural,' 'opposite' and 'complementary.' This notion crystallises heteronormativity in the sense that in heterosexual couples, women do things that men do not, and vice versa, and that taken together the chores of the respective genders will constitute a functional unit. However, heteronormativity is not a force that exists in itself, like gravity (even if it can sometimes feel that way). It exists only as far as human beings, or at least *enough* human beings, act according to its stipulations; it exists only to the extent that people *perform* stylised repetitions of acts (Butler, 1990) that confirm what is taken to already exist in advance. Performativity means that gender is based on endless repetition, or re-iteration.

The background in linguistics has contributed to some confusion about what Butler meant by gender performativity. Butler's book *Gender Trouble* (Butler, 1990) is sometimes regarded as one of the most ground-breaking texts in feminist theory, though it is widely debated. To some extent, Butler's subsequent book, *Bodies That Matter* (Butler, 1993) was a response to a critique that she faced after publishing *Gender Trouble*. This critique was based on the notion that Butler took for granted "that words alone ha[ve] the power to craft bodies from their own linguistic substance" (Butler, 1993, p. *xi*). By this, the critics assumed that Butler thought that it is the naming ('it's a boy/girl!') that brings gender into material existence. In fact, it is quite common that critics think performativity means that what is performed does not *really* exist, it is 'merely a social construction.' Nothing could be more wrong.

Butler's account was not only based on speech act theory, but also on Foucault's poststructuralist perspective. Foucault is famous for his specific conceptualisation of *discourse*. In English and many other European languages, discourse means written or spoken communication, or, colloquially, talking and writing. It sometimes refers to *authoritative* talk and writing about a certain subject. Foucault built on this mundane conceptualisation of discourse to mean something more. In one of his early books, *The Archaeology of Knowledge*, he defined discourse as "practices that systematically form the objects of which they speak" (Foucault, 1969, p. 54). Here, we can discern foundations of a theory of performativity. Objects are performed in and through historically constituted *practices*. However, it seems still that focus is essentially on speech practices, unless the 'speaking' is metaphorical and can mean something more. In a later text, Foucault developed the definition of discourse to include:

> the ensemble of more of less regulated, more or less deliberate, more or less finalized *ways of doing things*, through which can be seen both what was constituted as real for those who sought to think it and manage it and the way in which the latter constituted themselves as subjects capable of knowing, analyzing, and ultimately altering reality. These are the "practices," understood as a way of acting and thinking at once, that provide the intelligibility key for the correlative constitution of the subject and the object. (Foucault, 1998, p. 463; my emphasis)

In this definition, Foucault more clearly pointed out that 'practice' is not restricted to speech but can involve *all* practice: 'ways of doing things.' As Foucault's long-term companion Paul Veyne (2010) stated, "the object, in all its materiality, cannot be separated from the formal frameworks through which we come to know it" (p. 6). Moreover, in Foucauldian philosophy, acting and thinking should not be separated in the rationalist sense that 'first you think, then you act based on the thinking.'

Acting and thinking are parallel processes, or rather, thinking is a practice among other practices, partly with its own rules.

Based on Foucault's notion of discourse, then, gender performativity is about *ways of doing things in the name of gender*. Changing rooms, for example, are typically designated 'male' and 'female' through door signs. People do gender by entering either changing room, which may not only mean that they go through different doors; it may also mean that they enter slightly different practices that dominate the respective room. If so, then entering different changing rooms is also connected to separate ways of doing things, which in turn contributes to different experiences and, more importantly, to performing gender in differentiated ways. Butler suggests that performativity is a "reiterative power of discourse to produce the phenomena that it regulates and constrains" (Butler, 1993, p *xii*). In relation to competitive sports, the reality of gender does not precede the practices in which gender acquires its meaning. Rather, gender segregation in sports – which is sometimes supplemented by certain forms of differentiation of the sports practice, which I will illustrate in chapter 4 – is a discursive practice. It is a regulative and constraining practice that produces gender in particular ways.

Foucault and Butler took pains not to ignore the material aspect of gender and gendered bodies. They both emphasised that language, or culture, does not alone construct gender, but that language and matter – culture and nature – work together in the process. Still, criticism of an exaggerated focus on the role of language has constantly recurred. In recent decades, feminist theoretical physicist Karen Barad, for example, has offered new ways of dissolving the strict separation between language and matter. I will, however, not delve deeper into Barad's account here, but encourage interested readers to seek out Barad's article "Posthumanist performativity" (Barad, 2003) or their book *Meeting the Universe Halfway* (Barad, 2007).

Conclusion

Traditionally, gender – or sex – was seen as something created by nature. According to conventional narratives, nature created two sexes because this is a prerequisite for humans to be able to reproduce. Moreover, the same narrative holds that the sexes are also associated with distinct characteristics assumed to be 'natural' because they complement each other. These characteristics are sometimes thought to result from evolution. For some people, this assumed biological heritage justifies bringing up girls and boys differently and that, as adults, men and women have different tasks and chores. It also justifies keeping the sexes apart, where 'appropriate,' such as in sports and physical education. Sometimes the idea that nature can explain sex and associated behaviour is challenged by the idea that it is culture that produces gendered behaviour, that things like upbringing and the influence of other people, media, advertising, etc., affect the traits and capacities that people develop, including gender characteristics. No matter where you stand in this 'nature versus nurture' debate, within traditional ways of thinking about sex/gender, it is seen as a noun, a thing.

Ideas about gender contribute to injustice when they stand in the way of efforts to enable all people to live and work on equal terms. Sports and physical education are contexts where girls and women have gradually gained greater access. Sometimes, this access was conditioned by that the activities were 'adapted' in some sense to 'suit' girls and women. Oftentimes, however, the adaptation has also meant that male supremacy has been reinforced.

Various feminist efforts have been made to improve women's conditions in contexts that were previously closed to them: liberal, socialist, and radical feminism, for instance. These feminisms are also based on the assumption that gender exists as a noun, a thing.

Here, I have contrasted the conventional perspective of gender as something that people 'are,' with a perspective where gender is instead seen as a verb, something that people 'do.' The notion of 'doing gender' relates to gender performativity. In a sense, this perspective does not contradict that gender can have both natural and cultural backgrounds. What is important, rather, is how people do – or fail to do – gender in various social contexts. 'Failing' to do gender, which can also be seen as *queering* the practice, relates to expected behaviour in a social context, what constitutes the norms for how people are expected to act, for example based on whether they are assumed to be women or men. Gender norms are relationally created, often in terms of opposites: what men do, women do not do; what men look like, women do not look like; what men are good at, women are not good at; and vice versa. Such a perspective, and the possibility of queering the practice to subvert dominating norms, has much to offer in the critical study of sports and physical education.

Questions

- What does feminism mean, to you? Can you see yourself as a feminist?
- Can you distinguish the differences between the different feminisms described in the chapter?
- What does gender performativity mean if you were to describe it?
- How does gender performativity change the understanding of gender?
- How does gender performativity change the understanding of gender equity?

CHAPTER 4

Gender Performativity in Sports

Introduction

In this chapter, I will present examples of gender performativity in competitive sports. As outlined in chapter 3, gender performativity is affected by material, organisational, and social conditions that characterise the context where people are doing gender. The doing of gender is never unconditional. The material, organisational, and social framework of sports practice enable certain ways of doing gender, while disabling other ways.

The assumption that the genders should be kept apart in connection with competition probably sounds reasonable to most people. It would be considered unjust if women had to compete against men. At the same time, most people would also acknowledge that there is great intra-gender variation, meaning that women between themselves can be quite different and the same goes for men. This suggests that what is seen as fair is not only a matter of size, for example. In some situations, big men compete against small men, just as big women compete against small women. In some sports, such as wrestling and boxing, special competition classes are created to deal with these differences. Measurements are based on quantifiable characteristics, often weight. However, gender is a more elusive category, and the borders are more fluid. Unlike weight, where 70 kilograms is always more than 69 kilograms and less than 71, in the case of gender, there are few parameters that can be taken for granted. Most people put up with this ambiguity, probably because the category gender is assumed to be significant enough to warrant a separation.

Although the classification system in sports excludes more than two genders, social developments in recent decades show that more people either find it difficult to identify unambiguously with one gender or are excluded from belonging to a particular gender by others. More trans and intersex people have challenged the idea of two separate and binary genders. This is the theme of a later chapter (Chapter 6).

In the following, I offer three illustrations of gender performativity in sport. The first illustration concerns how various sports organise and regulate gender in their activities. This illustration highlights how material conditions, such as the design of equipment, contribute to gender performativity. The second illustration discusses gender patterns concerning participation in various sports. The final illustration concerns how sports are experienced by the participants, with a specific focus on gendered experiences.

Organising Gender

As I mentioned in the book's introduction, most of my examples are Swedish. This means that they do not automatically reflect situations in other countries. However, the point is not primarily to demonstrate 'how it is,' but to use the notion of gender performativity to understand 'why it is.' The situations I describe may not exactly reflect situations in other countries, but the principles of gender performativity are the same. The *doing* of gender can take place in diverse ways in different parts of the world. At the same time, it should be noted that sport rules and regulations, which are governed by international sports federations, are not receptive to cultural differences. They are the same all over the world and they are largely based on Western gender norms. In athletics, women compete in the 100 metres hurdles with hurdles that are 84 centimetres high all over the world, while men compete over 110 metres with 106.7-centimetre hurdles.

Analysis of regulations from all seventy federations in the Swedish Sports Confederation (Larsson & Johansson, 2012) showed that gender is constructed in four separate ways: 1) no gender division, 2) gender division, but no gender differentiation, 3) gender division and a quantitative gender differentiation, and 4) gender division and a qualitative gender differentiation.

1) *No gender division.* In sports such as equestrianism and motorsports, women and men often compete against each other in one competition class. Here, the genders are not separated, although performance can be quite physically demanding. A common competition class means that both men and women can win. Of course, there may be other ways people do gender, such as in terms of appearance, dress, demeanour, and more, but the sports regulations are constructed as gender neutral or non-gendered.

2) *Gender division, but no gender differentiation.* At first glance, it seems that many sports belong to this category, such as Nordic and alpine skiing, speed-skating, basketball, martial arts, shooting, and more. Here, women and men have separate competition classes, but arrangements are otherwise the same. However, a closer look at the regulations of most of these sports indicate that there are few sports that do not also include some sort of differentiation based on gender. I

will come back to these differentiations in the next two categories. One relatively new sport where there is no differentiation is floorball.[2] Consequently, in floorball, players are separated by gender, but the sport regulations do not differentiate the players in any further way according to gender.

3) *Gender division and a quantitative differentiation.* This category includes sports where women and men compete in different classes, *and* where there are certain 'adaptations' to either class. Since a common pattern is that the same adaptations that are applied to women are also applied to children and youth, it is the men's version of the sport that is normative. The men's version is the template and adaptations are made for other groups. A quantitative differentiation refers to a measurable adaptation. For example, men play football (soccer) with a size 5 ball, women play with a smaller size 4 ball; men throw a 7.26 kg shot put, women throw a 4 kg shot put; men play volleyball with a 2.43 metres high net, women play with a net 2.24 metres high, and so on. This arrangement contributes to performing gender based on standards considered normal for each gender.

4) *Gender division and a qualitative differentiation.* In some sports, mainly in ones that are popularly designated 'aesthetic' sports, such as artistic gymnastics, dance, and figure skating, the regulations require either a different focus of the performance, or the events of the sport are entirely different for the two genders. In artistic gymnastics, the events for women and men differ somewhat. Men compete in Pommel horse, Still rings, Parallel bars, and Horizontal bars, while

---

[2] Floorball is a sport that resembles field hockey, but is played indoors, with plastic sticks and a plastic ball. Additionally, the pitch and the goal are smaller. It is popular in Sweden and some other European countries, but unknown in others.

women compete in Uneven bars and Balance beam. Both genders compete in Floor exercise and Vault. In women's Floor exercise, the performance includes a music component. This differentiation contributes to performing gender in qualitatively different ways based on specific characteristics attributed to each gender. In competitive ballroom dancing and figure skating (at least in pair skating and ice dance), a woman and a man constitute a pair who compete against other pairs. Both dance sport and figure skating are governed by the same logic as artistic gymnastics, where men perform acts of strength or the active part (e.g., the man throws the woman in pair skating), while women perform acts of expression or the reactive part. This logic is further emphasised through differentiated attire.

The above analysis shows that in competitive mainstream sports (e.g., which are part of the Olympic program), gender segregation *and* differentiation mean doing "man" is to be active and normative, while doing "woman" means to be reactive and adaptive. As above, the mainstream understanding is that both categorisation (two genders) and differentiation (male: active; female: reactive) 'mirror' the order of nature. The theory of performativity, on the other hand, suggests that these cultural arrangements within competitive sports contribute to a process where various human beings are *normalised* according to the two main categories, each with their own specific characteristics constructed as *opposite* and *complementary*.

Taken together, this signifies not only gender but also *heteronormativity*. If people perform 'normal' gender, they are implicitly expected to be heterosexual, or 'straight.' Conversely, if people 'fail' to perform – or *do* – 'normal' gender, if they *queer* the practice, they may well be taken for homosexuals. While non-heterosexuality is not as stigmatised in some countries as it was some decades ago, there are still ample examples of how lesbian, gay, and bisexual people prefer to avoid coming out to avoid potential stigma and violence they may still be subjected to.

In this section, I have shown how competitive sports, through material and organisational properties, regulate gender performativity in particular ways. Athletes do gender in differentiated ways because of sports regulations. Material and organisational properties may include equipment, competition distances, valued characteristics in judged sports where a woman and a man compose a pair, and more. This way of doing gender has a profound impact on participation patterns.

Participation

In this section, my illustrations are based on participation patterns in Swedish sports. While sports participation in most countries expresses some kind of gender pattern this may vary between countries. However, the purpose of the section is not to establish who participates in which sports, or which sports are seen as masculine or feminine, but to examine the pattern over time in a particular context, and to discuss this pattern based on the perspective of gender performativity. Readers may then want to reflect upon participation patterns in their own specific contexts. In a first sub-section, I explore gendered participation patterns in terms of the breakthrough of various sports on a national level (Olofsson, 1989). By 'breakthrough,' I mean when different sports receive a significant increase in practitioners in a country or when a sport gets national championship status. In a second sub-section, I will explore how girls and boys, women and men are distributed in different sports at various ages (Larsson & Johansson, 2012).

Let me begin with the 'big history,' that is, when female participation breaks through on a broad front in diverse types of sports. It is a common pattern that sports were initially practiced by men. Having said that, as I stated in chapter 2, during the late 19th and early 20th centuries, women sometimes started to take up the same sports as men only to subsequently be banned from these sports. For example, a women participated in the second edition of the 90-kilometre cross-country skiing race *Vasaloppet* in 1923. However, her participation created debate and women were prohibited from starting in the race for the next 58 years. The same pattern exists in various other events, from the Olympics to recreational competitions. Some sports were originally designed for women, such as rhythmic gymnastics and synchronised swimming. Unlike the male dominated sports, however, there is still only marginal interest from boys and men in these sports. While women have started to participate in most sports originally pursued by men, there are still very few men participating in the latter sports. This pattern can be interpreted as an indication of the normativity of men's sports. This also means that while women can, at least under certain circumstances, 'do man,' it seems to be harder, perhaps more stigmatised, for men to 'do woman.' For men to participate in female-dominated sports could be a way to truly queer the activity.

While men dominated most sports up until the mid-20th century, the overall pattern is that women started to participate in individual sports (non-power and non-contact sports) in the 1950s, in team sports in the late 1960s and 1970s, and in power and contact sports (such as martial arts), as well as in motor sports in the 1990s. Ice hockey is a particularly interesting case. Unlike team ball sports, such as football and handball, which grew in popularity among women in the late 1960s and early 1970s, women's ice hockey had its breakthrough in the 1990s. Thus, participation in ice hockey resembles participation in contact sports rather than team ball sports. Moreover, when women start to take up a sport that was previously entirely dominated by men, there is debate around the possible noxiousness of this sport to women. For example, a particular focus is put on women's fertility if they participate in certain sports. This involves assumptions that strenuous physical effort 'masculinises' the female body and may make women infertile. Parallel to this debate, there is also widespread rumour that women who take up a previously male-dominated sport are lesbian. These examples highlight the close relationship between gender norms and heteronorms (Hargreaves, 1994).

Now I move over to the 'small history,' which is about participation patterns in different age groups (Larsson & Johansson, 2012). Concerning children aged 7-12 years when parental involvement is an important prerequisite for sports participation, boys and girls participate in gender stereotypical sports to quite an extent. For example, apart from football, the largest sport in Sweden among both girls and boys, small boys are relatively more frequent participants in various games, such as ice hockey, floorball, and tennis, while small girls participate to a greater extent in individual sports, such as equestrianism, gymnastics, and swimming. Some years later (at age 13-16), as the children develop some more autonomy, boys continue to participate in chiefly the same sports as before (football, ice hockey, floorball, and basketball), but girls start to take up games (handball, floorball, basketball). Even later (at age 17-20), while boys remain in the same sports, girls to some extent reorient from games back to individual sports (e.g., athletics and keep-fit activities), but not to the same sports they played as children.

The above pattern can be interpreted in the sense that at an early age, when parents control their children's sports participation, it seems to be important that girls and boys perform normalised (i.e., heterosexual) gender. Adolescence seems to be an age where, at least initially, gender loses its grip on children, or at least to girls. In the late teens, it seems again that normalised gender performativity is emphasised. It should be noted that while girls' sports participation is to a relatively greater extent characterised by mobility, boys' participation is instead characterised by stability. That is, while most boys stick to the sports they picked up at an early age, many girls try out a greater variety of sports. Again, this can be interpreted as a sign of the normativity of men's sports, which also means that the pressure is greater on boys compared to girls to perform normalised gender. In addition, it also signals that the fear of stigmatisation because of suspected homosexuality is smaller among girls compared to boys. This brings me over to the third and last theme: experience.

Experience

The above sections have illustrated how competitive sports, through material and organisational arrangements and participation patterns, contribute to regulate gender performativity according to a normalised framework where the genders are 'opposite and complementary' and where 'doing man' is normative, while 'doing woman' is adaptive/reactive. I will now devote attention to how sports participants experience this situation.

The examples mainly come from my own studies of Swedish youth sports. For nearly 30 years, I have conducted interviews with young athletes, typically between ages 15 and 20. My starting point is that what people experience is always 'right' but from a certain perspective (and it is impossible to imagine experiences that do not start from a certain perspective). For example, when badminton players Camilla and Cecilia in the below excerpt discussed their coach's actions during training sessions, my focus was not on whether the two girls are 'right' or not (cf., Larsson, 2021). Rather, my focus was on their experiences and how they make sense of the situation and the coach's actions.

> Camilla says: So, I can say one thing, and that was also with our coach on Wednesdays, once when I did wrong, when I played with Cajsa, a girl in our group, then he said: "If you do it right, maybe you can beat the boys too." Like I couldn't beat them anyway?! I got kind of angry, but I didn't show it.
>
> Cecilia interjects: Well, that's also one thing that I came to think of now, I don't know if it was when we had [the same coach], I think we had [another coach]. [...] Then it was like this that we had some fitness, and then it was like: "The girls can do five, the boys can do ten."
>
> Right, he was really rotten, Camilla confirms.

Indeed, I did not interview Camilla and Cecilia's coaches, so I cannot talk about how they experienced the situations that the two girls refer to. Arguably, it could have contributed to a more nuanced picture, but the point is not to ascertain who is right and who is wrong. The girls' experiences are themselves worthy of attention.

In a recent Swedish study (Larsson, 2021), leaders and coaches held that most girls 'naturally' embody values such as aesthetics and care, while boys 'naturally' embody values such as competition and aggression. Moreover, it was taken for granted that boys are better at sports and take competition more seriously. This perception was noticeable when sports leaders and coaches explained why girls and boys need to be separated in sports practice. These ways of reasoning about gender, which are consistent with previous research (Kempe-Bergman, *et al.*, 2020; Svender, *et al.*, 2012), chiefly follow what Messner (2011) termed soft essentialism (see chapter 1).

Soft essentialism is also expressed in leaders' and coaches' views of gender equity. In the above study (Larsson, 2021), I noted three approaches to gender. The first approach, *don't know – can't act,* means that club representatives express a passive approach to gender patterns and gender norms. The leaders and coaches were uncertain about what to do about gender norms – if anything at all. A wrestling coach voiced this approach in the following way (all quotes have been taken and translated from Larsson, 2021):

> We've felt that there's limited interest among girls, even though we're open to them, but we can't do much for them when they don't come. [...] After all, there's not much we can do about things.

A representative of another wrestling club expressed the same approach, although this time, most young wrestlers were girls. Nor could this leader point out what contributed to this pattern. The phenomenon can thus be the same regardless of whether it is boys or girls who dominate the business. The 'don't know – can't act' approach was articulated in several interviews. It included no explicit considerations about gender, which suggests that gender norms are in fact something of a non-issue to a lot of sport leaders and coaches. Relating the matter to the notion of soft essentialism, this approach is reasonable if you believe that participation patterns are the result of individual – and unconstrained – choice.

The second approach, *know – try to act,* means that club representatives have a more active approach to gender patterns and gender norms. This approach includes attempts to involve young people in systematic evaluation of the activity. Leaders and coaches who articulated a 'know – try to act' approach provided young athletes with opportunities to speak their mind. The following quote from an interview with two coaches in taekwondo illustrated this approach. A male coach introduced the notion of 'value-based clubs':

> **Male coach**: … it was probably about ten years ago that we sat down and decided that: "We'll become a value-based club." It's about equality, that it shouldn't matter what skin colour, religion, or gender you have. […] Partly it was about getting more female instructors at all levels. The choice of words, how to approach each other, is also extremely important. No one should feel offended […].
>
> **Researcher**: Do you take special measures to make this situation real?
>
> **Male coach**: Yes, it's a continuous work. Each semester, it's important to ask ourselves: what have we done well and what do we need to change? [...] Then it's very much that it should feel equal, safe, secure. Nobody should feel outside… We have women who practice in niqab, several religions together… a lot of different people. These are questions we ask ourselves several times each semester and think about what we can do better.
>
> **Female coach**: It's very mixed, really. My athletes represent all kinds of religions, ages, genders, skin colours and...
>
> **Male coach**: … sexualities.
>
> **Female coach**: Yes, sexualities too.
>
> **Male coach**: A boy has come out [as gay] quite recently ... and he said that it feels very safe here.

The 'know – try to act' approach was, however, uncommon among club representatives in this study, which suggests that systematically offering young athletes' opportunities to speak their mind is not commonplace in Swedish club sports (see also Redelius & Eliasson, 2022).

The third and last approach is *know – but reluctant to act,* which means that coaches and leaders acknowledge gender but hesitate to intervene in gender patterns. Below is a quote from a coach who, however reluctantly, felt forced to take some measures to provide equitable conditions to both girls and boys in the club:

> We don't assume anything regarding gender ... just as we don't assume anything in relation to what skin colour people have, or what they believe in. [...] When I work with group composition, I want everyone to have fun and stay in the club. And that means that you sometimes must put on other glasses [...] Though I don't see myself as having a normative function or telling girls that they should hang out with boys or vice versa or mix. I know that these girls are better off in that group, yes, then it must be like that. I arrange a girls' night and then I think a bit like this: "This is probably damn affirmative action", so it's far from my own picture of how I'd like to have it. But it's clear, gender and age are something that I can consider.

Although the quote highlights awareness of possible injustice due to gender, in this case that girls need to be supported by affirmative actions, the coach underlined that he would prefer not to have this 'normative function.' He favoured embracing what he believes is a gender-neutral approach, although he also admitted to not living up to this aspiration. A leader from another club reasoned in similar ways:

> Now we've deliberately decided that we need more girls (female leaders) as role models. ... I'm not that keen on pursuing this gender politics [...] I'd prefer to lift out that paradigm completely, but somewhere you still must ... live in the reality. So, female role models, absolutely.

This leader seemed to find some merit in affirmative action, but he was also reluctant to play any part in what he refers to as 'gender politics.' This suggests that gender issues occupy a tenuous position among some coaches and should preferably be avoided in their minds. In fact, several club representatives were explicitly negative about trying to change gender patterns. They could not see why gender was something to consider in their activities. The following is a quote from an ice hockey coach:

> ... this gender debate that's going on ... you can say different things about it. Is there actually any interest among girls [to play hockey]? When I grew up, the girls weren't interested in playing hockey. Still, they had the same possibilities as me to go out on a frozen lake and skate and play. So, this basic interest, I don't know if the girls have it. [...] Then, why small girls play with rabbits while boys play with a puck and a stick; that probably goes back to well before you and I were there.

This coach seemed to assume that everyone had the same opportunities to pursue their interests in the same effortless manner as he did. His reasoning can be articulated as: 'since it was easy for me, it would be as easy for anyone else'. Taking one's own experiences as universal can lead to symbolic violence – non-physical violence manifested in power differentials between social groups. Symbolic violence means that the norms of a hierarchically superior social group are assumed to apply also to a subordinate group (Bourdieu and Wacquant, 1992). In the case of competitive sports, symbolic violence occurs when the conditions that apply to boys and men are also assumed to apply to girls and women.

Few young athletes voice concerns related to gender. There could be many ways to interpret this fact. It could mean that gender is, in fact, a non-issue. Or it could be because it can be difficult to articulate experiences rooted in symbolic violence. Some, however, like Camilla and Cecilia, appear very clear-sighted. Camilla articulated a concern that the coach took for granted that she could not beat the boys, although she did not reveal this concern to the coach. Cecilia continued to say, while at the same time eyeballing me, that:

> now it's getting a little feminist, but why couldn't the girls do as many (repetitions) as the boys? I know the boys have more mus-

cles and so, I understand that biology, but then, why couldn't we do that also? [...] Sometimes when I play with some boys in our group they say, "I didn't hit it as hard as I could" and "I let you win", and so, and then I also get angry. It feels like I'm getting mad at everything now.

To become 'a little feminist' is apparently not highly valued to these girls, although they seem to experience a need to use feminist countermeasures against symbolic violence. The girls' account highlighted that since the notion 'boys are better at sports' is unwittingly embodied among their coaches; it becomes problematic for the girls to challenge it without being regarded as 'angry feminists.' The interview excerpt mirrors an indignation felt by girls as they are subjected to what they believe are unfair generalisations, since they experience marginal, if any, opportunities to question such generalisations.

Conclusions

In the previous chapter, I outlined the general foundation for understanding gender in sports in terms of performativity or doing gender. I started this chapter by pointing out that gender performativity is never unconditioned. Athletes do gender to a great extent along the required frames that policy, organisation, and material properties promote. The competitive sports framework promotes athletes doing gender according to four alternatives depending on the sport: a) no gender, b) gender division but no gender differentiation, c) gender division and a quantitative differentiation, and d) gender division and a qualitative differentiation. Essentially, binary gender becomes intelligible within these four ways of doing gender in sport, which also reflects heteronormativity.

In Participation, I gave an overview of gender patterns in various sports over time (from the turn of the century 1900 until modern times) and the life course (from childhood to adulthood). Based on these statistics, I concluded that the norms that regulate gender performativity change over time, both historically and with increasing age. An overall pattern was that while women have gradually found their way into men's sports, men have not found their way to women's sports. I interpreted this as an expression of a hierarchy between masculinity and femininity; a hierarchical relationship that suggests 'doing man' represents the all-inclusive category of 'human,' while 'doing woman' only represents 'woman.' In the world of sports, women can 'do man' to a greater degree than men can 'do woman' without risking stigmatisation, marginalisation, and exclusion. However, this comes with a price, namely that girls' and women's achievements in male dominated sports tend to be diminished and – sometimes – ridiculed.

In the last section, I gave examples of how girls and boys, women and men, experience the gender orders of sports and how experiences of these orders affect how athletes do gender. These examples indicated an overall pattern that young people playing sports relate to a general assumption that 'boys are better at sports' and that this norm must not be questioned. Coaches, for their part, seem to prefer not to intervene in gender patterns, but from time to time it happens that they do so anyway, should the injustices become too apparent. However, at such times, the 'adjustments' that are made tend to perpetuate rather than challenge and change the notion that 'boys are better at sports.'

Questions

- To the extent that you have experience of sports participation, how well do you recognise yourself in the description of sports' gender patterns and how young athletes do gender in sports?
- Do you have experiences of doing gender in unexpected ways in some sport?
- Have you experienced injustice in sports?
- Have you tried to point out this injustice to coaches or managers?
- What response did you get?

CHAPTER 5

Gender Performativity in Physical Education

Introduction

In this chapter, the focus is still on empirical examples of gender performativity, but I now shift from sports to physical education. Thus, the chapter is about how students and teachers do gender in this subject, but just like in the previous chapter it is also about the material, organisational, and social conditions that produce gender patterns in certain ways. While sports are both formally and informally influenced by the gender binary inherent in the two competition classes, Swedish schools are governed by legislation and governing documents that stress how society, including school, shapes assumptions about gender. Rather than an essentialist understanding of gender, in Messner's (2011) terms, this signals a constructionist understanding.

The Swedish Education Act (2014:960) stipulated that schools and teachers must "counteract discrimination and in other ways promote equal rights and opportunities in the field of education regardless of gender, gender identity or expression, ethnic affiliation, religion or other belief, disability, sexual orientation or age." Under the Education Act, the National curriculum states that all discrimination "must be actively counteracted," and that the school "has a responsibility to make visible and counteract gender patterns that limit students' learning, choices and development" (SNAE, 2022a, p. 5-6). It is clear that school staff, to an even greater extent than sports leaders and coaches, are responsible for making visible and counteracting gender patterns. However, the state also tasks physical education teachers with teaching *about* gender norms. Among secondary school physical education content is:

> Norms around different kinds of activities. How norms affect individuals' participation, for example norms around gender and functionality linked to various movement activities. (Lower secondary school; SNAE, 2022a, p. 50)
>
> Ability to ethically take a stand on issues of gender patterns, equality and identity in relation to sports and exercise. (Upper secondary school; SNAE, 2022b, p. 1)

It follows from this that physical education teachers need to understand both how they counteract gender patterns in the subject and how they teach students about gender norms in ways that do not reproduce them.

Research shows that many gender patterns that pervade sports are also found in physical education (Solmon, 2014). The main interpretation is that sport activities are on the schedule in physical education to such an extent that finding the same gender patterns is inevitable. In many countries, the legislated distinction between leisure time, sports, and school physical education is not as strong as in Sweden and other Nordic countries. Nevertheless, it is clear from the research that the difference is not as distinct as intended in practice (Larsson, Fagrell & Redelius, 2009; Oliynyk, 2021). Furthermore, as I will illustrate in this chapter, physical education classes are strongly influenced by heteronormativity (Larsson, Redelius & Fagrell, 2011), but there is still a lack of Swedish research on how LGBTQI+ students experience the subject. In international research, however, it is clear that LGBTQI+

students are marginalised (Berg & Kokkonen, 2022; Dévis-Dévis, et al., 2018; Landi, et al., 2020).

In the previous chapter, I illustrated how the rather explicit structure concerning how gender is regulated in various sports affected gender performativity. In physical education, however, there is not the same clear structure, but there is still reason to highlight how teaching and lessons are structured more generally and how this affects gender performativity.

Organising Gender

As noted in chapter 2, the background of physical education in most (Western) countries can be found in military and health-related motives during the 19th century. Physical education was supposed to prepare (older) boys for military service and to counteract the unsanitary consequences of urbanisation and sedentary lifestyles among (younger) boys and girls. The method employed for this purpose was Swedish gymnastics, a group-oriented type of gymnastics where the students moved in pre-determined drills commanded and monitored by a gymnastics director. During the mid-1900s, Swedish gymnastics was largely replaced by sports activities and play, and sometimes dance and outdoor activities. However, as Kirk (2010) has noted, a lesson structure consisting of teacher-led and highly decontextualised sport techniques taught – and assessed – in short lesson sequences (typically one to three lessons) remained.

The structure of this 'molecularised' version of physical education (Kirk & Houssin, 2021) means that students are introduced to a number of rules and set techniques they are to practice before they can participate in the 'whole' activity. For example, students are introduced to individual passes, dribbles, and shots in a particular ball game, which are subsequently followed by pair exercises and small team games before they play the 'full' game. In fact, this lesson structure also dominates other content, such as dance and outdoor activities. Typically, any content is allowed only brief time, between one and three lessons, before new content is introduced. This is because teachers often feel that 'there is so much to cover,' that 'students soon find it boring,' or that 'there must be something for everyone' during the schoolyear. Such a 'smorgasbord' of activities (Tinning & Fitzclarence, 1992) means that students are allowed only minimal time for practice and consequently cover content that is "an inch deep and a mile wide" (Kirk, 2010, p. 7). Additionally, student performances are typically assessed based on set, yet often implicit, standards derived from competitive sports.

The molecularised version of physical education has profound consequences for how gender can be performed in physical education classes. Since around 1980, co-education is the dominating practice in Swedish physical education. Co-education was to prevent students from being socialised into traditional gender roles and because girls and boys were not separated in any other subject. The transition from gender separate teaching to co-education meant that what girls and boys previously did separately (and still do separately in club sports), they now did together. However, the introduction of co-education chiefly meant that boys *and* girls were offered much the same content that was previously part of *boys'* physical education curriculum – with the addition of one or two occasional dance lessons. This has prompted Kirk (2002) to talk about not only a molecularised, but also a 'masculinised' version of physical education.

In the masculinised version of physical education, lessons are dominated by various ball games and fitness activities. Dance and outdoor activities may also occur, but this seems to quite some extent to be up to individual teachers to decide. This is an overarching pattern in many countries (Pühse & Gerber, 2005). However, while in some countries (arguably, where classes are still gender divided), competition elements seem to be uncontroversial in physical education, in other countries, such as the Nordic countries, competition is considered incompatible with the educational purposes of physical education. This means that the explicit motive for including ball games must be something other than to nurture competitiveness. Typically, in Nordic and some other countries, ball games are supposed to foster *cooperation*. However, the elements of cooperation seem to be taken for granted, because the molecularised practice is focused on individual technique rather than on collaborative elements of games. In the context of playing the 'full game', only limited attention is paid to teamwork (or cooperation).

More generally, the molecularised and masculinised version of physical education means that girls and boys are expected to develop fitness and movement skills in sports dominated by boys, but unlike in competitive situations outside schools, girls and boys are expected to practice these sports together in physical education. Moreover, when the students are assessed, they are assessed based on set standards taken from men's sports that must be 'adapted' for girls. This partly forms the basis for the gender patterns identified in physical education. Such patterns include that *more* boys (rather than 'the boys') find the subject meaningful and participate wholeheartedly, while *more* girls (rather than 'the girls') have difficulty seeing the point of the subject and may participate with some hesitation. The responsibility to counteract these patterns means that teachers need to interpret them as in fact *possible* to counteract. This means that teachers need to understand *why* gender patterns exist in ways that make it reasonable to challenge and change them. The question is, *how do* physical education teachers understand gender patterns?

Teacher Experiences

In my own studies of physical education teachers' understandings of gender patterns in physical education, there are some recurring themes: a) 'activity first,' b) 'it's – not – about sport,' and c) 'you can't affect it.'

'*Activity first.*' Clearly, a lot of teachers see their primary task as offering students opportunities to be physically active and preferably in joyful ways. Below are the words of two teachers whom I had the opportunity to talk to some years ago (cited from Larsson, Fagrell and Redelius, 2009, p. 7):

> **Teacher 1**: The goal [of physical education lessons] is a multitude of activities, comfort and joy of movement. That they [the pupils] can try a lot, that's really important. And that it'll be fun.
>
> **Teacher 2**: Most pupils think it's fun. That's when I feel satisfied, after such a lesson, when I know that everyone participated, everyone laughed, had fun.

The first teacher's account also illustrated the dominance of the 'smorgasbord' version of physical education, that the students should meet 'a multitude of activities.' The same pattern occurred in a subsequent interview study about how teachers develop movement capabilities among students (Larsson and Nyberg, 2017, p. 141).

> **Teacher**: … you must have the opportunity to practice; you can't just roll out a ball; you must have a chance to bounce the ball and, if you do lay-ups: what foot you should start with, so that you learn a pattern of movement … […] but I do that just

> because I have to make assessments, it doesn't matter anyway, the main thing is that they move, but I can't think like that when I'm supposed to assess them, can I?

The teacher first acknowledged that it was difficult for students to develop movement capabilities if there was no time for practicing only to then emphasising that *how* students move is not really of primary importance, but *that* they move. In fact, this study indicated that teachers felt that having to teach movement capability restricted students' opportunities to be physically active. Gunn Nyberg and I interpreted this to reflect a feeling among teachers that resulted from set and narrow, yet chiefly implicit, standards of pre-determined movements; standards that seep into physical education from competitive sports – which brings me over to the second theme.

'*It's – not – about sport.*' As teachers emphasise a multi-activity and joy of movement approach, they also emphasise that physical education is not about competition and that measuring physical performances has no place in the subject.

> **Teacher**: It's not that important to me that the pupils can do well in long jump or running, but more to make it an experience, and the one who wants to can practise more. I've taken away watch and tape measure (Larsson, et al., 2009, p. 8).

A lot of teachers wish to distance physical education from competitive sports, to instead offer a joyful and recreational opportunity for movement. This approach has its limitations, however, if the teachers' *wishes* are not backed by changes in teaching practice. For example, observational studies (e.g., Redelius, Quennerstedt and Öhman, 2015) suggest that teachers devote little time to communicating *what is* the aim of physical education and the various movement activities introduced. Rather, when talking about these activities, the teachers use a 'sport language' to communicate the subject, much like the teacher in the excerpt below. At the beginning of a lesson, the teacher gathered the students to explain the upcoming lesson:

> **Teacher**: Listen up! Today, I have basketball ... and then on Friday I have handball ... and then after the lesson on Friday, there'll be a tournament.

In another class, on another occasion, a student asked the teacher:

> **Student**: What'll we do today?
>
> **Teacher**: We'll do volleyball today.

While many teachers emphasise that physical education is *not* about competitive sports, at the same time they signal competitive sports by using sports language and practices (e.g., tournaments and names of competitive sports). Thus, Swedish physical education teachers seem to perceive themselves as involved in a pedagogical project that does *not* involve competitive sports. They do not see competition as compatible with their assignment as physical education teachers. Nevertheless, the use of sports language and practices taken from competitive sports strongly contribute to reproducing the same gender patterns in physical education as those in competitive sports. While teachers believe that physical education is *not* about competitive sports, as I will show shortly, students still interpret physical education practice as tantamount to just that.

'*You can't affect it.*' The above situation gave rise to clear gender patterns, but many teachers seem to have a tough time acknowledging that they themselves contribute to this situation through their pedagogy, including language use and selection of activities. Some teachers were able to see the connection:

> **Teacher**: Well, I think that ... I think the personality of some teachers has favoured boys. Since you measure and take time and such. That's what I think [...] and maybe that the range of activities favours boys.
>
> **Teacher 3**: I think that, generally, it's the norms of the tough guys that govern the lessons. It's the tough, hard guys who set the rules, and most girls come to heel. (Larsson, et al., 2009, p. 10)

Other teachers, however, explained the patterns based on properties within the students that cannot be changed:

> **Researcher**: Have you reflected on why you should move away from traditional gender patterns? [...]
>
> **Teacher**: Good question. I probably actually don't think so. [...] Some things are genetic, I personally think. (Larsson, et al., 2010, p. 68; author translation)

When gender patterns are interpreted as expressions of, for example, genetics, the focus shifts from how teaching affects student behaviour to how they (the students) 'are.' Consequently, teachers sometimes hand over to the students to decide how teaching is to be arranged:

> **Teacher**: When it comes for example to football, I ask the girls if they want to play mixed or for themselves. Yesterday I had a class that wanted to play separately while others wanted to play mixed. I listen to them. (Larsson, et al., 2009, p. 9; author translation)

Worth noting here is that the teacher lets the girls decide, indicating that this is the subordinate group. However, it is not something that the teacher reflects on further. It is enough that the girls have been given the opportunity to choose how they want to organise themselves. Some teachers are reluctant to intervene in behaviour that they interpret as 'natural.' Here, such behaviour concerned 'rowdy boys' and 'cautious girls:'

> Teacher: Because if it's about ball games, the boys would have to hold back, and the girls might not dare to set about themselves. Most girls don't. They hide from the ball, and they're afraid of being hit hard by it, or of not getting a pass. Then both would be losers. [...] We have differences in strength and ... if you collide with a boy. There are biological differences after all. [...] I think that much is genetically and biologically inherited. We are different sexes, and we react differently on different things. Men still have this hunter instinct ... I really believe it's inherited. (Larsson, et al., 2009, p. 10; author translation)

To these teachers, counteracting gender patterns appeared unreasonable. Rather than because of their own pedagogical considerations, these teachers understand boys' and girls' behaviour as biologically determined and thus impossible to change. By referring to innate behaviour, some teachers abdicate their responsibility to counteract traditional gender patterns.

Student Experiences

How do students experience physical education and how do they perceive gender patterns? First, it should be noted that physical education is one of the most appreciated subjects in Swedish schools, although this drops at around 15 years of age. This is a time when many things converge, for example: 1) participation in (competitive) club sports decline, 2) performance requirements increase in school, including in physical education, and 3) at least statistically, physical differences between girls and boys increase. Despite many teachers offering 'a multitude of activities, comfort and joy of movement,' some students struggle to find secondary school physical education meaningful. However, as recent research showed, statistically, it is not certain that girls view physical education more negatively than boys (Jansson, et al., 2022).

More generally, scepticism towards physical education is partly derived from the fact that students are more visible to each other compared with other school subjects, and therefore are open to comments about appearance and performance. An overarching pattern is that while both girls and boys may well have opinions about each other's appearance and performance, it is mainly (some) boys who publicly exclaim these opinions. Thus, the dominating norm in this context is that while girls must hold back their opinions, the same does not apply to boys. A similar pattern occurs when it comes to who are allowed to make jokes with sexual connotations:

> **Interviewer**: sometimes there's talk about it being a game of some kind … perhaps not an explicitly sexual game, but at least something that resembles it … […] Is there any sign of such things in your class?
>
> **Girl**: Well, they do that sort of thing quite a bit, but it's only a joke.
>
> **Interviewer**: They, who are they?
>
> **Girl**: The boys … well, not all boys of course, but some. I don't feel, you know, as if I'm being … undressed, or threatened.
>
> **Interviewer**: No … What do they joke about then?
>
> **Girl**: No, but they … their jokes can be very crude [giggles].
>
> **Interviewer**: Aha [chuckles], dirty jokes you mean?
>
> **Girl**: Yes.
>
> **Interviewer**: Okay.
>
> **Girl**: Yes, and start tickling … I don't know … there's nothing sexual about that.

> **Interviewer**: Nooo, well, it depends on how you look at it, but, um, they get hold of you?
>
> **Girl**: Yes, sometimes, but it's only a joke, and I don't think anybody minds.
>
> **Interviewer**: No, but do any of the girls fight back?
>
> **Girl**: No.
>
> **Interviewer**: Not at all?
>
> **Girl**: Nobody wants to. (Larsson, et al., 2011, p. 72)

This student asserts that 'the game' under scrutiny in the interview is not really a sexual game, but 'only a joke.' In fact, according to the student, 'there's nothing sexual about it.' And yet there is, but girls and boys do not seem to participate in it on equal terms. Girls cannot or should not want to push it. The 'rules of engagement' do not only concern the sexual game. A 16-year-old girl talked about her experiences of physical education lessons:

> **Interviewer**: It's clear that the boys claim more space and are more active, especially when playing dodgeball ... and as you say [...] they throw harder and so on [...] Do you think that matters, or that it has a positive or negative impact or whatever?
>
> **Girl**: No, well, I don't think that it matters very much...Um... I mean it doesn't do me any harm [giggles].
>
> **Interviewer**: Do you think that you ... have fewer possibilities to show ... the teacher what you can do then?
>
> **Girl**: No because I think that I can do that anyway ... Well ... eh ... No, I don't think so. I mean, it's not as though they ... If I really wanted to, I could play really aggressively and ... be a boy [giggles] ... but I don't feel the need for it.

> **Interviewer**: Neat expression: 'be a boy,' what does it mean exactly? [both chuckle]
>
> **Girl**: Naah, but I mean, throw hard … fling the ball. (Larsson, et al., 2011, p. 77-78)

This student was quite explicit that to 'play aggressively' is tantamount to 'be a boy' in this context. 'Real boys' are expected to play this way, and girls should preferably not even 'feel the need for it.' My and my colleagues' (Larsson, et al., 2011) interpretation is that ball games exhibit the same structure as the sexual game above. Both highlight the heteronormativity of physical education lessons. Playing ball and making dirty jokes are then closely interconnected, but what happens if the activity is something completely different? Below, another student reiterated the gendered rules, but in connection with another activity. When talking about pair dancing, the interviewer asked whether the students themselves could pair up or if the teacher did this:

> **Girl**: No, it's the teacher … he pairs us up.
>
> **Interviewer**: Does that feel okay?
>
> **Girl**: Yes.
>
> **Interviewer**: Is that better than having to choose a partner yourself?
>
> **Girl**: If you have to choose your own partner, it's usually the girls who ask the boys. Otherwise, nothing happens … because the boys never ask us … the girls.
>
> **Interviewer**: It's a bit awkward then?
>
> **Girl**: Yes … I mean … [giggles] when you dance with someone they think, they imagine that you're in love with them, but you're not … it's not about that, love … you're only dancing. (Larsson, et al., 2011, p. 75)

Apparently, dance seemed to induce almost an opposite behaviour compared to ball games; a behaviour where it is boys who need to not push it if they do not want to get lost in the swamp of heteronormativity (see also Forestier & Larsson, 2023).

Queering Physical Education Teaching

A major trend in research is demonstrating how heteronormativity is reproduced, much like in the examples above. Recently, however, examples of how heteronormativity is challenged – or queered – have become more common. The following incident during a physical education lesson may indicate possibilities for queering teaching (Larsson, et al., 2014). As was discussed in chapter 1, the notion of queering designates deliberate attempts to actively subvert traditional gender patterns. Importantly, queer teaching may allow students to challenge heteronormativity in the subject, given that the teacher is open to this influence. The incident happened in a grade 9 class (students aged 15-16) that was about to start the second lesson of a schottische dancing unit. Schottische is a traditional Swedish folk dance. During the previous lesson, the teacher taught the techniques of the dance, the 'steps and spins,' through direct instruction to students who danced boy-girl. Now, as the second lesson is about to start, four girls approached the teacher. They were reluctant to participate: what's the point of learning schottische, nobody dances it anyway? Why can't they dance Zumba instead? And why do they have to dance with the boys? The teacher tried not to clash with the students, but instead to deliberate. He answered their questions thoughtfully (the quotes below are from Larsson, et al., 2014, pp. 142-143):

> **Teacher**: Why must girls and boys dance together? Because we normally do that…dance boys and girls.

The girls' objections continued. The teacher, for his part, followed a line of reasoning in which dance is associated with heterosexual partner relationships. The following quote illustrates the girls' response:

> **Girl 1**: Perhaps I'm a lesbian?
>
> **Girl 2**: I'm also a lesbian.
>
> **Girl 3 and Girl 4**: Me too.
>
> **Girl 2**: Then you want to dance with a girl.

These queries made the teacher more confused, but still not confrontational. Instead, he tried to listen to the students:

> **Teacher**: Okay…(hesitantly).
>
> **Girl 1**: Are you with us? Do you understand?
>
> **Teacher**: Yes, I do understand. (still slightly hesitantly)
>
> **Girl 2**: I think Anna has a good point here.
>
> **Teacher**: Yes…one doesn't have to dance boy and girl. That's right. It's my heterosexual norm that haunts me here!
>
> **Girl 1**: Exactly!

As a result of this conversation, the teacher radically changed his teaching. The students got the opportunity to dance regardless of which gender was represented in the pairs. Since the previous lesson involved the students learning 'boy and girl steps,' they now had to take a step back in the learning process to explore schottische anew. Among other things, strong norms regarding gender and sexuality associated with dance surfaced, thus becoming possible to discuss explicitly among the students. My colleagues and I concluded that this event may offer clues about how teachers and students can collaborate to queer physical education lessons more broadly (Larsson, et al., 2014). The teacher abandoned the teacher-centred and linear approach of 'steps and spins' as the 'best way' for students to acquire pre-determined and decontextualised schottische skills. Instead, a more exploratory and experimental teaching and learning emerged, also offering possibilities to challenge heteronormativity (Kumashiro, 2004).

Conclusion

The focus of the present chapter has been to highlight how teachers and students do gender in school physical education. In fact, at least in Sweden, schools and teachers are tasked to both counteract traditional gender patterns and teach students about gender norms. In practice, physical education is at least partly permeated by the same gender patterns as sports and one reason for this is that many traditional sports are also found in physical education, without the educational purpose of these sports being fully clarified. The students usually experience it as if they should 'do sport'. Moreover, little time is devoted to specific content and after just one or two lessons, students' performances are assessed. This molecularised lesson structure creates tight frameworks that circumscribe how students can (un)do gender.

Many teachers in physical education are aware that lessons are permeated by gender patterns, but they sometimes seem reluctant to attempt changing these patterns because they are seen as 'natural' and therefore impossible to change. Furthermore, it appears to be difficult for teachers to fundamentally change teaching if the view of physical education as a smorgasbord of activities dominates. However, I was able to demonstrate one example of how teaching can change. Instead of a teacher-centred technical approach, one teacher implemented a student-centred exploratory approach, which allowed other patterns to be established, including some that queered the practice.

On the surface, physical education may seem gender-neutral. This is partially true, but observations of lessons and interviews with students show that the framework for how boys and girls can act during physical education lessons may be narrower than what appears on the surface. There are clear norms for how girls and boys should look, move, and act in various movement activities.

Questions

- How well do you recognise yourself in the description of gender patterns in physical education?
- Do you have experiences of doing gender in unexpected ways during physical education lessons?
- Have you experienced gender injustice in physical education?
- Have you tried to point out this injustice to teachers?
- What response did you get?

CHAPTER 6

LGBTQI+ Issues in Sports and Physical Education

Introduction

Since at least the 1990s, research into gender in sports and physical education has been supplemented by research into how lesbian, gay, bisexual, transgender, intersex, and more (LGBTQI+) individuals experience heteronormative sport and physical education cultures. Such an approach is well in line with the theoretical perspective in focus of this book: the theory of gender performativity. This theory does not assume that gender 'is' anything specific, but that gender is always in a process of becoming in various practices and contexts. There are also opportunities to do undo, or to *queer*, gender. This chapter is precisely about how people sometimes queer gender within sports and physical education contexts.

Lesbian, Gay, and Bisexual People's Experiences of Sport

This section is based on parts of Eva Linghede's doctoral thesis *Glitching sport (science): a criticalcreative inquiry of queerings in Swedish sport (science)* (Linghede, 2019). As Linghede's supervisor, I was involved in a study that concerned lesbian, gay, and bisexual people's experiences of participating in elite sports (Linghede and Larsson, 2017). In this study, 13 individuals volunteered to take part in research interviews. 'Elite' was defined by the research participants having represented a Swedish national team at competitions or matches at international level. Recruitment of research participants began with the researchers searching for 'coming-out stories' in the media. Elite athletes who had come out publicly as lesbian, gay, or bisexual were contacted and asked about their interest in participating in a research interview. All volunteered to participate.

The recruitment prompted a discussion between researchers and participants regarding what the research was about. Or perhaps rather, *who* the research was about. Initially, we used the phrase 'elite sports persons who *are* lesbian, gay, or bisexual.' However, some of the persons that we approached problematised the notion that you 'are' once and for all lesbian, gay, or bisexual. It may be that during different periods of a lifetime, people might understand themselves in different ways. For this reason, we searched for individuals who had experiences of same-sex relationships during their elite sports career, regardless of how they identified themselves at the time of the interview.

The analysis of the 13 interviews resulted in three narratives, which were designated *Figuring a Sports Dyke*, *Figuring a Sport Fag*, and *Figuring a Sexuality Which is Not One*. We borrowed the notion of *figuring* from the research of Braidotti (2011) and Haraway (2004). It means that the narratives are based partly on 'what is' – what the research participants said during the interviews – and partly on 'what could be.' The 'what could be' is the result of an elaboration of occasions during the interviews when the research participants were apologetic about their sexuality. For example, some of them emphasised that they did not want to appear overly demanding and challenging and therefore sometimes held back about their sexual preferences. Instead, we reversed these occasions to celebrate queerness.

Figuring a Sports Dyke is about Ebba, who participated in several world championships in ice hockey. She started her career playing on a boys' team, where she had to 'put up with' a lot of bantering among her teammates who repeatedly bragged about their (hetero)sexual conquests in the changing room.

> *Ten years later she sits in a different changing room. The boys' hockey team has been replaced with a women's team, but they're still talking about girls. Felicia and Molly, two of the younger players on the team, are talking and laughing out loudly. [...] Their conversation almost embarrasses her. She can't help but think that maybe things are hardly any more civilized in girls' changing rooms than they are in boys'. On the other hand, she does appreciate the openness she's always encountered in ice hockey. She's never had to "come out" in any of the teams she's played for. It's always been understood that some people like girls and some like guys. To be honest it's more surprising when someone talks about male partners and lovers. And surely her teammates living straight have to put up with occasional taunting's – as well as invitations – one might add. Admittedly with a wink, but still. The other night her wife actually confronted her about this and asked, "Shouldn't you be a bit more open minded and say 'her' OR 'him' about any partners when you talk with the younger players, just so they feel that either is just as okey? After all, being a lesbian is hardly a requirement, is it?" She considered this for a while but then thought: hell no! Even if it isn't a requirement to be a lesbian, what is wrong with assuming that the younger players like girls? It is almost as if you are saying that desiring women is not a good thing then. And for all she knows, it is a very good thing indeed"* (Linghede and Larsson, 2017, p. 296f, original italics).

In the article, we (Linghede and Larsson, 2017) concluded that this narrative "resonates with studies that have gone beyond demonstrating that some sports attract lesbians and serve as a lesbian and subcultural field to argue that sport can facilitate and nurture the expression of nonconventional sexualities" (p. 297). In this narrative, sports dyke Ebba did gender repeatedly in the 'wrong,' or queer way; she celebrated homosexual relationships, and she actively decided to contest heteronormativity: what is wrong with assuming that girls (can) like girls? In the next narrative, *Figuring a Sports Fag*, sports fag Pontus, who participated in elite track and field, also queered gender:

> They're stretching, lying in the grass while watching the other athletes as they move around in the sports ground. "Listen, Pontus," Erik says all of a sudden, "that guy over there, in green jersey, do you think he's got a nice butt?" He is looking toward the running track. Pontus starts laughing. This really must be one of the great things about doing athletics: all the hot bodies. He takes a good look at the guy in the green jersey and says: "Well, yes, I guess so, but he isn't really my type." "So I thought," says Erik and sounds pleased, "he is more my kind of guy." Pontus smiles and reflects that he's never enjoyed being in a club the way he does now. Even if he's been quite open in his earlier clubs he feels as if he has been censoring himself in the context of sports. It's as if he has been trying to be little more of a "guy" than he really is, in the way he moves, in his tone of voice and his choice of topics for discussion. He never really wants to talk too much about himself being gay because he didn't want the others to feel uncomfortable. But at the same time it was about his fear of not being allowed to be a member of the group. […] Thinking about this really pisses him off. By adjusting his looks and behavior he realizes that he has accepted rather than challenged homophobia.

The *Figuring a Sports Fag* narrative "goes beyond acceptance and tolerance talk where you are welcome *even* if you are gay, but where you still should not be *too much* gay in the way you move, talk, and act" (Linghede and Larsson, 2017, p. 300). Much like sports dyke Ebba, sports fag Pontus repeatedly queered gender through his doings; he embraced the possibilities of being homosexual in a sports context. As such, he "enacts a queering elsewhere beyond heteronormativity, where you do not have to think about being accepted or not by the majority culture." However, as I indicated above, it is not certain that you 'have' one sexuality once and for all. The third and last narrative, *Figuring a Sexuality Which Is Not One*, highlighted that during different periods of a lifetime, people might identify themselves in different ways. In this narrative, Alma problematised the heterosexuality-homosexuality binary.

> "What are you saying? Have you met a guy!?" Talia is staring at her and can hardly keep herself from laughing. "Have you joined the other team? What does that make you?" "Yes, who or what is she really? Here and now, is she a heterosexual? Or a bisexual? But it doesn't feel as if she is having a relation specifically with a woman or a man. An individually sexual maybe, would that be allowed? Some years ago when she realized that she liked girls this quite soon became part of her identity. A very positive part. And later as she got some attention in mass media, that identity became stronger because she had to stand for it in public. But this had to be rethought when she met Petter. One of the first thoughts that struck her was "what will people think now?" […] What disturbs her […] is that it's more difficult to open up the normative eyes of others now that she's having a relationship with a man. Now, when someone just assumes she has a boyfriend, she can't contradict them by saying she has a girlfriend, and if she brings her boyfriend to a martial arts competition or a Christmas party with the club, she will be absorbed into heteronormativity like most of the others. She's much less visible now. She's also got a slight feeling that the LGBT-community thinks of her as a traitor. If you were celebrated for coming out as a lesbian – is it really OK to then be with a man?

In 'Figuring More Livable Elsewheres,' we (Linghede and Larsson, 2017, p. 302) suggest that "Alma's story illustrates that people's experiences are often far more fluid and complex to be squeezed into one box only and that their sexual *re*orientations disturb dominant ideas of sexuality *as* identity." Alma's ways of doing gender repeatedly subverted the notion that one's sexual identity is stable, or fixed. She showed how it is possible to queer, or not queer, at different times in life. However, the narrative also showed that even what *is* queer may vary. Once you have come out as a lesbian, it may be even more queer to engage in a heterosexual relationship. Taken together, the three narratives, *Figuring a Sports Dyke*, *Figuring a Sport Fag*, and *Figuring a Sexuality Which is Not One*, illustrated that heteronormative sport culture frames the experiences of people with all kinds of sexual preferences, that homosexuality can be not only tolerated but celebrated, and that it should not be taken for granted that a person 'have' one stable sexual identity throughout life.

Trans Issues in Sport

I now proceed from the LGB (i.e., lesbian, gay, and bisexual) to the T (i.e., trans) of LGBTQI+. *Trans* includes "individuals who have a gender identity other than that which was assigned to them at birth as well as those who may not entirely identify with a particular sex" (Love, 2014, p. 376). Importantly, trans is not a homogeneous phenomenon. While some transgender individuals may seek medical procedures, such as surgery or hormone therapy to transition to a particular gender, others may not wish to seek such procedures. In contrast to transgender, the term *cisgender* refers to "individuals who have a match between the gender they were assigned at birth, their bodies and their personal identity" (Schilt & Westbrook, 2009, p. 461). Transgender people have contributed to challenge conventional thinking about gender separation in sport. As more trans people are visible in society, the question arises as to whether binary gender should be regarded as 'natural' or if culture forces binarity on nature. Nature instead appears to be much more diverse.

The attention of trans has, much like intersex, contributed to some debate in relation competitive sports. The inclusion of trans people, above all trans girls and women, has in some countries stirred up a sometimes-heated debate (McClearen, 2022; Parry & Martínková, 2021). Sometimes, (e.g., Pike 2021) attempts are made to distinguish between (biological) sex and (sociocultural) gender identity. From a performativity perspective, however, such a distinction is problematic. Biology is not more fundamental than culture; they create each other in the sense that it is heteronormativity that performs both.

In 2021, I initiated a research project about transgender people's experiences of sport and exercise. Much like in Linghede's study about LGB athletes' experiences of elite sport, some of the research participants in this project challenged my assumption that you 'are,' once and for all, a 'trans person.' To some, perhaps most often trans people who undergo gender affirming procedures, a trans identity is developed during a certain period of their life, but that later in life has only a marginal significance. Others, perhaps people who identify as non-binary, may refrain from attempting to identify themselves based on gender altogether. Eventually, and like the approach in Linghede's study, this project involved people who at some point in their lives had perceived themselves as trans (Larsson & Auran, 2023).

Unlike in Linghede's study, however, the focus was not specifically on elite sports, but more broadly on competitive and recreational sports as well as fitness. Ten individuals volunteered to take part in research interviews. Two major themes from the interviews will be presented here. First, how trans identities are partly performed in relation to gender equity initiatives in sports; second, how trans individuals must work systematically to facilitate their own inclusion.

The first theme, *how trans identities are performed in relation to gender equity initiatives* grew based on an observation that trans identities are not fixed nor finished. Rather, they grow gradually without a clear start and end. Bellamy, for example, said that:

> I was at the gym a couple of times, and that was before I had landed entirely in myself. In what I was. But I knew I'm not a cis-hetero-man, but I'm somewhere on the LGBTQ scale, sort of.

The experience of 'being somewhere in the LGBTQ scale' was also highlighted by Hollis, who described the process even more clearly as a gradual process towards 'insight' where sports participation and its constant gender separation functioned both as a catalyst for this insight and, sometimes, as a source of irritation and frustration:

> I played basketball in high school […] and during that period, I came out as a lesbian, or first as bisexual and then as a lesbian. Then I started to notice in relation to sports that […] I became more and more [a] trans guy.

Bellamy and Hollis were around 30 years of age. Arguably, it was more important to them to 'discover,' or 'establish,' their identity than to Gray, who was well into his 60s. Gray was the only research participant who replied 'doesn't matter' when asked about their preferred pronoun:

> **Isak**: How do you identify yourself?
>
> **Gray**: I don't. Well, of course, I have an identity, but I refrain from dressing it in one of two words, because it only adds to a lot of things to it with which I may not agree. […] In a way, I'm happy that I didn't fall within what was then defined as trans, because I don't identify myself as such. I just said that I'm not a girl.

Gray referred to a career within bodybuilding, a context that at least some decades ago allowed participants to avoid committing themselves to a specific gender identity or to a specific trans identity. This 'in between' position, neither cis nor trans, offered Gray a sense of freedom to participate in body building – and build a body – without necessarily having to adhere to set norms and body ideals. Unfortunately, Gray adds, the situation in gyms that he benefitted from several decades ago has now changed for the worse. Most contemporary gyms are completely permeated by mainstream culture's heteronormative messages regarding bodies and appearance.

The gender division common in sports, which was discussed in chapter 4, affects the experiences of trans persons in particular ways. Several research participants voiced annoyance with what they see as a constant focus on gender segregation that takes place not only in competitive sports but is also commonplace in fitness and recreational sports. Gender separation is particularly poignant in relation to trans identities because trans people often find this arrangement problematic. Several of the research participants problematised gender separation. Cleo, for instance, said that:

> It's a giant colossus to change the rules. Why does this rule exist? (Referring to gender segregation in child sport). When you go to international competitions and those regulations, you can't influence those if the whole world doesn't want to take part (referring to gender division in elite sport). […]
>
> **Isak**: What do you think would need to change for trans people to participate in sports and exercise to the same extent?
>
> **Cleo**: That you have 'child sports;' that you don't talk about boys' and girls' football, but that it's children's football. That you don't divide in any way, at least not until you're 12. […] In some sports you wouldn't even have to divide at all.

To a lot of trans persons, gender segregation is unintelligible. They perceive it as perfunctory practice and a major obstacle to trans inclusion. Given that society imposes two genders, on the other hand, gender segregation can also be seen as a gender equity measure; a purposefully implemented practice aimed at levelling the playing field for the underrepresented gender. One gender equity measure, for example, is the need for Swedish sports clubs to register the number of participating girls and boys to receive their state subsidy. Cleo's view of this arrangement:

> Everything you report is based on gender; on how many participants there are in different activities. And it's so stupid!

Thus, separatist ventures can be seen as double-edged swords in the pursuit of inclusion. What makes a certain arrangement in a particular practice inclusive for some may be exactly what makes the practice exclusive for others. That is, while gender segregation may contribute to include cis persons of an underrepresented gender, it may exclude trans persons. The issue of inclusion, and more specifically how trans individuals routinely must work systematically to facilitate their own inclusion was the second theme in the study.

Swedish sport is dominated by a self-belief that 'everyone is welcome.' However, sports clubs and other sports facilities, including commercial gyms, seem to have a tough time living up to this assertion when trans people knock on the door. Moreover, inclusion seems to be conditioned depending on how the trans persons queer the activity – how they *do* trans. Overall, the research participants described their inclusion as either by creating 'their own' queer spaces or passing *as if* they were cis persons. Consequently, there were few ways for trans individuals to fully participate in mainstream sports activities where they do not have to excuse their presence among cis persons.

How do trans persons facilitate their own inclusion? This depends on what resources they have available. Personal characteristics could become such resources. For example, Arden, who identified as non-binary, often flew under the radar in the sense that few noticed their non-binary identity if they did not make it explicit. They were typically interpreted as a cis woman. However, Arden described how difficult it was to exist at the gym or at the bathhouse as a non-binary person. These spaces postulate two genders (and nothing in between) and to some extent Arden had to give up on themself before they could exercise there.

Another 'asset' for inclusion was the ability among the trans persons to 'pedagogically' and non-confrontationally prepare people in the sports club or at the fitness centre for their participation – and to teach others about being trans. This way of proceeding in a non-confrontational manner was related to the 'sort' of trans identity that the person displayed. Trans men and non-binary persons, like Arden, seemed to have it easier to speak in a non-confrontational way. To non-binary Eddie, it was a way to both avoid harsh treatment and make their non-binary identity clear from the beginning:

> Because my problem, or what to say, is that I become invisible, and I must work myself to become visible so that people use the correct pronoun and so on. Because that's my need, not to be invisible in my trans identity in new contexts. [...] Some just want to fly under the radar, but I can't if it means that I become invisible.

While Eddie found it problematic to be made invisible in their trans identity, in other cases, the problem was rather the other way around, i.e., that the trans identity caused too much attention. This was particularly the case with trans women, who needed to develop yet another 'asset': conformity. This meant that if the trans persons refrained from displaying 'too much' anger and frustration they were more easily welcomed in the club activities. Four of the research participants displayed anger about the conditions for participation in sport and exercise in the interviews. Two of them, Hollis and Indigo, chose to quit their sports (respectively, boxing and football/soccer) before any conflict emerged. Billie and Dylan, however, chose to inform their clubs about their needs – with disappointing results. Trans woman Billie reported:

> I came out and ... told people I had trained with for many years: "Hello, I'm the same person as you've always known but I have a different pronoun and I thought that, like in a week or so, I will start changing among, well, in the women's' changing room." And then the club kicked back and, yes ... God, it's been a real affair. But, yes, they forbade ... they called to lots of meetings where they forbade 'exposed male genitals,' was probably their first formulation. And then, yes, they said that everyone's welcome at the training, but it's an extra offer to be allowed to change at the club.

Because of this, Billie, like many other trans persons, were forced out from participation in sport during the transition period.

Many of the challenges and opportunities that characterise trans people's involvement in sport recur when it comes to intersex people's involvement in sport.

Intersex Issues in Sport

Intersex includes individuals with "atypical combinations of chromosomes, hormones, genitalia, and other physical features" (Buzuvis, 2011, p. 11). As I have described earlier, sports – and competitive sports in particular – are organised based on binary gender as a structuring principle. Conventionally, women and men are so different in physical aptitude and performance that separate classes are justified to ensure a level playing field (with some exceptions, e.g., in equestrian sports). As above, often rigid gender divisions make it difficult for people who do not want to – or who cannot – adapt to this arrangement to participate. While being trans is about people whose gender identity differs from the gender they were assigned at birth, *intersex* describes persons who have innate variations in their gender characteristics that do not correspond to how typically female or typically male bodies are expected to be. Intersex variations can be about anatomy, hormonal, or genetic differences, which means that intersex individuals are sometimes unaware about their intersex condition. The phenomenon is known world-wide, but at least in industrialised countries a single gender is often established early in life, sometimes through medical (including surgical) intervention. In non-industrialised countries, it is more common that individuals grow up without undergoing medical intervention.

One intersex phenomenon is called *hyperandrogenism*, which according to the Karolinska Institute medical dictionary refers to a condition caused by an excessive secretion of androgens in the body which affects men only marginally, but which contribute to develop male secondary sex characteristics in women. While the phenomenon is frequently pathologized in medical discourse, as gender is interpreted within a strictly binary framework where the genders are 'binary and complementary,' some biologists, such as Fausto-Sterling (2000), claim that gender exists on a floating scale and that it could be useful to talk about a diversity of genders. Rather than pathologizing the phenomenon, this would make intersex conditions normal and expected variations among humanity. In Fausto-Sterling's account, while 'nature' exhibits a diversity of sexes, culture places people into two seemingly homogeneous gender categories: women and men. In relation to this, Linghede (2018) saw intersex existence as a 'promise,' something that gives people the opportunity to think and act differently in relation to preconceived social categories.

Linghede (2018) theorised the promise of intersex with the help of the concept *glitch*, which "usually refers to a minor malfunction or defect in modern technology, a sudden unexpected event, an error in a structured system" (p. 575). However, regarded as a promise, glitch can be seen as "the other side of technology," or even a "celebration of broken technologies" (Sundén, 2015, p. 6), something that has the potential to help people get out of what is taken-for-granted. Linghede (2018) used the notion of glitch to analyse a letter written by the Indian sprinter Dutee Chand to the Athletic Federation of India in September 2014 after her disqualification from participating in athletics due to her hyperandrogenic condition.

> The high androgen level produced by my body is natural. I have not doped or cheated. If I follow the IAAF guidelines you have attached I will have to undergo medical intervention in order to reduce my naturally produced androgen level. […] I feel perfectly healthy and I have no health complaints so I do not want to undergo these procedures because the experts also tell me they are likely to have side effects. […] Also, I am unable to understand why I am asked to fix my body in a certain way simply for participation as a woman. I was born a woman, reared up as a woman, I identify as a woman and I believe I should be allowed to compete with other women, many of them whom are either taller than me or come from more privileged backgrounds, things that most certainly give them an edge over me. (CAS 2014, 8, 9; quoted in Linghede, 2018, p. 572).

Ironically, Chand was thus asked to dope herself to be able participate in the women's competition class. She raised the question why her condition would disqualify her from participation, while other conditions such as body size, training conditions, and other forms of performance enhancement are readily allowed. In this way, Chand highlighted a few power-related circumstances. First, she pointed out that the competition class 'women' is not only, or primarily, about ensuring a level playing field. Its primary function is rather about regulating gender. However, regulations do not typically aim at things that are *possible* to influence and could contribute to level the playing field, such as to limit injustice based on where athletes grow up and train and the resources available in these contexts. Rather, they aim at things assumed to be self-evident (such as gender) but turn out *not* to be – apart from the use of doping. Second, Chand's protest made explicit that only women are examined and required to show a 'correct' gender in sport. This never happens to men, something that could signify that while nature organises gender along a horizontal axis with floating boundaries, culturally the genders are organised according to a vertical axis with clear boundaries. That is, while intersex can be interpreted as a natural variation among humans, sport's two competition classes allow no "in between." Along the vertical axis, the category man is at the top, which means that no male athletes whose athletic success is based on genetic benefits are required to dope themselves to be eligible to participate in the male competition class. On the other hand, this is precisely what happens to female athletes who live under the same conditions.

Both trans and intersex persons must show culturally acceptable indications that they 'belong' to one of two binary genders before they are accepted in competitions. At least, this is the case if they wish to participate as women. This signifies that the category 'woman' is not only hierarchically inferior to the category 'man,' but that the category woman is also to a greater extent scrutinised and regulated based on ideas about what belonging to this category means.

Conclusion

Sports and physical education are strongly affected by heteronormativity, which includes a strictly binary view of gender. This means that participants must perform gender in specific ways to gain entry. As more people challenge society's gender norms when they fail or do not wish to perform gender in expected and culturally 'appropriate' ways, it has become increasingly difficult to perpetuate the notion that heterosexuality and 'opposite' genders are self-evident. Even biological research has pointed out that gender is a dynamic phenomenon with fluid boundaries around genders and sexualities. Research shows that biology exhibits a significantly greater diversity regarding what can be seen as 'natural' than what culture acknowledges. Rather, culture seems to limit diversity. This becomes evident in the case of Dutee Chand. Her story challenges the fixation in sports that there 'are' two genders that must be kept apart. However, the solution is probably not to simply remove the two competition classes. Presumably, other, and more versatile arrangements are necessary to ensure inclusive and equitable participation for all.

I began the chapter by reflecting on how, with the help of research and imagination, we can imagine possibilities for queering sports culture – to undo gender or do gender differently. Queering sports means more than just identifying the effects of heteronormativity and binary gender, but also challenging and changing the order of things. In the chapter, I highlighted how we can figure sports dykes and fags who do not apologise for their existence and who stand up for their opportunities to play sports on their own terms, without the requirement that they must adapt to be included. Moreover, I showed possibilities to figure a sexuality which is not one in the sense that people should not be required to demonstrate one coherent and unchanging sexual orientation.

On the contrary, the stories point to opportunities to love and live with different (kinds of) people, in connection with sports.

I also demonstrated how trans and intersex identities are performed and experienced as both enabling and hindering within binary sports culture. Bellamy, Hollis, Gray, and more, discovered their transness in relation to sports culture's expectations that people should be heterosexual and one of two genders. However, transness is not only a disadvantage, but can also allow participation in sport and exercise in different and border-crossing ways. Gray, for example, could both pass as male and present a more ambiguous and border-crossing persona depending on the situations they participated in. Conversely, Dutee Chand asserted her right to participate despite her inability to fit into the two-gender model of sport.

Questions

- What are your experiences of heteronormativity and the requirement to display binary gender in a sporting context?
- What possibilities do you envision in terms of the possibilities of including LGBTQI+ people in sports?
- Regardless of if you identify as LGBTQI+ or not, how can you examine your own responses to homophobia and transphobia in sports?

CHAPTER 7

Conclusions
And the Way Forward

The purpose of this book was to explain the significance of studying gender and sexuality in sports and physical education. Moreover, the purpose was also to illustrate what the notion of *gender performativity*, or *doing gender*, can contribute relative to other approaches to gender and gender equity. One, perhaps implicit, ambition of the book has also been to point out a need for the continued struggle for gender equity and inclusion in sports and physical education. Even though some may think we have reached an equitable situation where everybody is welcome to participate, there are still obvious signs that this is not the case. There are still many who experience marginalisation and exclusion from sports and physical education, and opportunities and resources enjoyed by certain groups do not apply to everyone. In this book, I have offered the notion of gender performativity as a conceptual tool to understand gender and work with gender equity in these contexts. In this concluding chapter, I will close the book with some thoughts about what the future might hold.

What About the Future?

To predict the future is impossible. And every attempt to predict the future can be seen as an attempt to enact that future. Therefore, it is probably better to discuss the critical questions that arise because of the perspective I have presented in this book. One important question is, of course, whether the notion of gender performativity will play a significant role in future work with gender equity and inclusion. Here I think we can already see that this perspective has had influence by raising new questions that have been able to change sports and physical education practice, at least to some extent, as is indicated in some of the chapters. Today, there is greater readiness than before to discuss and problematise exclusion and to work for equity and inclusion of previously marginalised and excluded groups. On the one hand, this seems easier within the framework of physical education compared to sports. This is likely because physical education is not primarily aimed at comparing individuals' physical performances with each other and therefore does not require the binary gender division to be maintained. On the other hand, work for inclusion seems to some extent to be easier in sports compared to physical education because what it means to be 'good' at sports is clear. The aim of physical education is sometimes not so clear, such as what it means for students to be 'good' at physical education. In countries where a stronger division between sports and physical education is made, such as in the Nordic countries, uncertainty about the purpose of the subject and what it means to be 'good' at physical education contributes to reproducing traditional gender patterns. I therefore see good opportunities for sports and physical education to continue developing into inclusive practices using the perspective of gender performativity.

At the same time, I must admit that I see clouds of worry gathering. While progressive democratic values that embrace diversity and focus on inclusion and equity are held in high regard in many countries and contexts, there are other countries and contexts where conservative, even downright reactionary views are being enforced. Since sports and physical education cannot be separated from society at large, *where* people move will play a significant role in whether the positive trends that I reflected in the previous paragraph will continue. The conservative reasoning I have in mind is expressed not least when it comes to new anti-abortion laws, changes in legislation regarding non-heterosexual marriages and a generally stricter view of homosexual partnerships and eliminating the opportunities for trans and intersex people to live authentically. After all, knowledge can be a valuable tool in the fight for all people's rights to live and act according to their dreams, wishes and conditions, including when it comes to participation in sports and physical education. Hopefully, this book can contribute to increasing knowledge about gender, gender equity and inclusion in sports and physical education and what the gender performativity perspective can offer for continued positive development.

Questions

- What opportunities and challenges do you see with using the notion of gender performativity in your work?
- What challenges related to gender equity and inclusion do you perceive, now and in the future?
- What are the critical questions of today – and of the future – regarding sports and physical education?

REFERENCES

Aggerholm, K., Standal, O., Barker, D. M., & Larsson, H. (2018). On practising in physical education: Outline for a pedagogical model. *Physical Education and Sport Pedagogy*, *23*(2), 197-208.

Anderson, S. (2020). Bodying forth a room for everybody: Inclusive recreational badminton in Copenhagen. In: N. Dyck & E. Archetti (Eds.), *Sport, Dance and Embodied Identities* (23-54). London: Routledge.

Arnold, P. J. (1979). *Meaning in movement, sport, and physical education*. London: Heinemann.

Austin, J. L. (1962). *How To Do Things With Words*. Cambridge, MA: The William James Lectures.

Barad, K. (2003). Posthumanist performativity: Toward an understanding of how matter comes to matter. *Signs: Journal of Women in Culture and Society*, *28*(3), 801-831.

Barad, K. (2007). *Meeting the universe halfway: Quantum physics and the entanglement of matter and meaning*. Durham, NC: Duke University Press.

Berg, P., & Kokkonen, M. (2022). Heteronormativity meets queering in physical education: The views of PE teachers and LGBTIQ+ students. *Physical Education and Sport Pedagogy*, *27*(4), 368-381.

Birrell, S. (1984). Studying gender in sport: A feminist perspective. In N. Theberge & P, Donnelly (Eds.), *Sport and the sociological imagination* (125-135). Fort Worth, TX: Texas Christian

University Press.

Bourdieu, P., & Wacquant, L. J. (1992). *An Invitation to Reflexive Sociology*. Chicago, IL: University of Chicago press.

Braidotti, R. (2011). *Nomadic theory: the portable Rosi Braidotti*. New York, NY: Columbia University Press.

Brickell, C. (2003). Performativity or performance? Clarifications in the sociology of gender. *New Zealand Sociology, 18*(2), 158-178.

Butler, J. (1990). *Gender Trouble. Feminism and the subversion of identity*. New York, NY: Routledge.

Butler, J. (1993). *Bodies That Matter. On the discursive limits of "sex"*. New York, NY: Routledge.

Butler, J. (2004). *Undoing Gender*. New York, NY: Routledge.

Buzuvis, E. E. (2011). Transgender student-athletes and sex-segregated sport: Developing policies of inclusion for intercollegiate and interscholastic athletics. *Seton Hall Journal of Sports & Entertainment Law, 21*, 1-59.

Carli, B. (2004). *The making and breaking of a female culture: The history of Swedish physical education 'in a different voice'* (PhD dissertation). Gothenburg: University of Gothenburg.

Cavanaugh, J. R. (2015). *Performativity*. Oxford University Press.

Connell, R. W. (1983). *Which way is up? Essays on sex, class and culture*. London: Allen & Unwin.

Crum, B. J. (1993). Conventional thought and practice in physical education: Problems of teaching and implications for change. *Quest, 45*(3), 339-356.

Devís-Devís, J., Pereira-García, S., López-Cañada, E., Pérez-Samaniego, V., & Fuentes-Miguel, J. (2018). Looking back into trans persons' experiences in heteronormative secondary physical education contexts. *Physical Education and Sport Pedagogy, 23*(1), 103-116.

Barlow, F. K. (2019). Nature vs. nurture is nonsense: On the necessity of an integrated genetic, social, developmental, and personality psychology. *Australian journal of psychology, 71*(1), 68-79.

Elias, N., & Dunning, E. (1986). *Quest for excitement. Sport and leisure in the civilizing process.* London: Blackwell.

Engels, F. (1909, originally published in German in 1884). *The Origin of the Family, Private Property, and the State.* Chicago, IL: Charles H. Kerr & Company.

Fausto-Sterling, A. (2000). The five sexes, revisited. *Sciences, 40*(4), 18-25.

Firestone, Shulamith (2003, originally published in 1970). *The Dialectic of Sex: The Case for Feminist Revolution.* New York, NY: Farrar, Straus & Giroux.

Forestier, A., & Larsson, H. (2023). Choreographing gender: Masculine domination and heteronormativity in physical education. *Sport, Education and Society, 28*(2), 132–143.

Foucault, M. (1972, French original published in 1969). *The archaeology of knowledge and the discourse on language.* New York, NY: Pantheon Books.

Foucault, M. (1998). Foucault. In J. D. Faubion (Ed.), *Michel Foucault. Aesthetics, Method, and Epistemology* (459-463). New York, NY: The New Press.

Goffman, E. (1976). Gender display. *Studies in Visual Communication, 3*(2), 69-77.

Griffey, D. C. (1987). Trouble for sure a crisis—perhaps: Secondary school physical education today. *Journal of Physical Education, Recreation & Dance, 58*(2), 20-21.

Guttman, A. (2004). *Sports. The first five millennia.* Amherst, MA: University of Massachusetts Press.

Hall, M. A. (1988). The discourse of gender and sport: From femininity to feminism. *Sociology of sport journal, 5*(4), 330-340.

Haraway, D. (2004). *The Haraway Reader.* New York, NY: Routledge

Hargreaves, J. (1994). *Sporting females: Critical issues in the history and sociology of women's sport.* London: Routledge.

HCHR (2019). Fact sheet: Intersex. https://unfe.org/system/unfe-65-Intersex_Factsheet_ENGLISH.pdf

Hovden, J. (2010). Female top leaders–prisoners of gender? The gendering of leadership discourses in Norwegian sports organizations. *International Journal of Sport Policy and Politics, 2*(2), 189-203.

Jannini, E. A. et al. (2010). Male Homosexuality: Nature or Culture? *The Journal of Sexual Medicine, 7*(10), 3245–3253.

Jansson, A., Sundblad, G. B., Lundvall, S., Bjärsholm, D., & Norberg, J. R. (2022). Gender Differences and Inequality? A 20-Year Retrospective Analysis Based on 39,980 Students' Perceptions of Physical Education in Sweden. *Journal of Teaching in Physical Education, 42*(2), 371–382.

Kempe-Bergman, M. (2014). *Man talar om jämställd idrott: Om jämställdhetssamtal med manliga idrottsledare och förutsättningar för jämställd idrott* (PhD dissertation). Stockholm: The Swedish Sport and Health Sciences, GIH.

Kempe-Bergman, M., Larsson, H., & Redelius, K. (2020). The sceptic, the cynic, the women's rights advocate and the constructionist: male leaders and coaches on gender equity in sport. *International Journal of Sport Policy and Politics, 12*(3), 333-347.

Kirk, D. (1992). *Defining Physical Education. The Social Construction of a School Subject in Postwar Britain.* London: Routledge.

Kirk, D. (1996). The crisis in school physical education: an argument against the tide. *ACHPER Healthy Lifestyles Journal, 43*(4), 25-27.

Kirk, D. (2002). Physical education: A gendered history. In D. Penney (Ed.), *Gender and Physical Education* (36-50). London: Routledge.

Kirk, D. (2010). *Physical Education Futures.* London: Routledge.

Kirk, D., & Houssin, E. (2021). Beyond Molecularization: Constructivist, Situated and Activity Theory Approaches to Movement Learning. In H. Larsson (Ed.), *Learning Movements. New perspectives of movement education* (46-60). London: Routledge.

Kohl, H. W., Craig, C. L., Lambert, E. V., Inoue, S., Alkandari, J. R., Leetongin, G., & Kahlmeier, S. (2012). The pandemic of physical inactivity: global action for public health. *The Lancet, 380*(9838), 294-305.

Kumashiro, K. K. (2004). Uncertain beginnings: Learning to teach paradoxically. *Theory Into Practice, 43*(2), 111-115.

Landi, D., Flory, S. B., Safron, C., & Marttinen, R. (2020). LGBTQ Research in physical education: a rising tide? *Physical Education and Sport Pedagogy, 25*(3), 259-273.

Larsson, H. (2021). The discourse of gender equality in youth sports: a Swedish example. *Journal of Gender Studies, 30*(6), 713–724.

Larsson, H., Fagrell, B., Johansson, S., Lundvall, S., Meckbach, J., & Redelius, K. (2010). *Jämställda villkor i idrott och hälsa med fokus på flickors och pojkars måluppfyllelse*. Unpublished manuscript. Stockholm: The Swedish School of Sport and Health Sciences.

Larsson, H., Fagrell, B., & Redelius, K. (2009). Queering physical education. Between benevolence towards girls and a tribute to masculinity. *Physical Education and Sport Pedagogy, 14*(1), 1–17.

Larsson, H., & Johansson, S. (2012). *Genus och heteronormativitet inom barn-och ungdomsidrott. Könsmönster i idrottsdeltagande och regelverk inom idrott*. Stockholm: The Swedish Sports Confederation and The Swedish School of Sport and Health Sciences.

Larsson, H., & Larsson, B. (2023). Social stratification of physical activity. An exploration into how logics of practice affect participation in movement culture. *Physical Education and Sport Pedagogy, 28*(3), 213–228.

Larsson, H., & Nyberg, G. (2017). 'It doesn't matter how they move really, as long as they move.' Physical education teachers on developing their students' movement capabilities. *Physical Education and Sport Pedagogy, 22*(2), 137-149.

Larsson, H., Redelius, K., & Fagrell, B. (2011). Moving (in) the heterosexual matrix. On heteronormativity in secondary school physical education. *Physical education and sport pedagogy, 16*(1), 67-81.

Lewis, P., Benschop, Y., & Simpson, R., 2018. Postfeminism: negotiating equality with tradition in contemporary organisations. In: P. Lewis, Y. Benschop, & R. Simpson (Eds.), *Postfeminism and Organization* (3-18). London: Routledge.

Linghede, E. (2018). The promise of glitching bodies in sport: A posthumanist exploration of an intersex phenomenon. *Qualitative Research in Sport, Exercise and Health, 10*(5), 570–584.

Linghede, E. (2019). *Glitch i Idrottslandet: en kritiskkreativ undersökning av queeranden inom svensk idrott (svetenskap)* (PhD dissertation). Stockholm: The Swedish School of Sport and Health Sciences.

Linghede, E., & Larsson, H. (2017). Figuring more livable elsewheres: Queering acts, moments, and spaces in sport (studies). *Journal of Sport and Social Issues, 41*(4), 290-306.

Ljunggren, J. (2000). The masculine road through modernity. Ling gymnastics and male socialization in nineteenth-century Sweden. *European Sports History Review*, 2, 86–111.

Love, H. (2014). Queer. *Transgender studies quarterly, 1*(1-2), 172-176.

Lundquist Wanneberg, P. (2004). *Kroppens medborgarfostran: kropp, klass och genus i skolans fysiska fostran 1919–1962* (PhD dissertation). Stockholm: Stockholm University.

Loland, S. (2000). *Idrett som akademisk fag: fra grunnlagsproblemer til praktisk politikk*. Unpublished manuscript. Karlstad: Karlstad University.

McClearen, J. 2022. "If you let me play": girls' empowerment and transgender exclusion in sports. *Feminist Media Studies*, 1-15. doi. 10.1080/14680777.2022.2041697

Marshall, J., & Hardman, K. (2000). The state and status of physical education in schools in international context. *European Physical Education Review*, 6(3), 203-229.

Messner, M. (2011). Gender ideologies, youth sports, and the production of soft essentialism. *Sociology of sport journal*, 28(2), 151-170.

Millett, K. (2000, originally published in 1970). *Sexual Politics*. Urbana, Chicago: University of Illinois Press.

Oliynyk, I. (2021). *"Man vill ju ha med sig alla eleverna i undervisningen": Didaktiska val och genusmönster i skolämnet idrott och hälsa* (PhD dissertation). Växjö: Linnaeus University.

Olofsson, E. (1989). *Har kvinnorna en sportslig chans? Den svenska idrottsrörelsen och kvinnorna under 1900-talet* (PhD dissertation). Umeå: Umeå University.

Parry, J., & Martínková, I. 2021. The logic of categorisation in sport. European *Journal of Sport Science,* 21(11), 1485-1491.

Pike, J. 2021. Safety, fairness, and inclusion: Transgender athletes and the essence of Rugby. *Journal of the Philosophy of Sport,* 48(2), 155-168.

Pühse, U., & Gerber, M. (Eds.). (2005). *International comparison of physical education: Concepts, problems, prospects*. Aachen: Meyer & Meyer Verlag.

Redelius, K., Quennerstedt, M., & Öhman, M. (2015). Communicating aims and learning goals in physical education: Part of a subject for learning? *Sport, Education and Society*, 20(5), 641-655.

Schilt, K., & Westbrook, L. (2009). Doing Gender, Doing Heteronormativity: "Gender Normals," Transgender People, and the Social Maintenance of Heterosexuality. *Gender & Society*, 23(4), 440–464.

SNAE (1994). *Läroplan för det obligatoriska skolväsendet, förskoleklassen och fritidshemmet Lpo 94* (National curriculum for nine-year compulsory schooling, 1994). Stockholm: Swedish National Agency of Education.

SNAE (2022). Läroplan för grundskolan, förskoleklassen och fritidshemmet (National curriculum for nine-year compulsory schooling, 2022). Stockholm: Swedish National Agency of Education.

SNSB (1962). *Läroplan för grundskolan* (National curriculum for nine-year compulsory schooling, 1962). Stockholm: Swedish National School Board.

SNSB (1969). *Läroplan för grundskolan* (National curriculum for nine-year compulsory schooling, 1969). Stockholm: Swedish National School Board.

SNSB (1980). *1980 års läroplan för grundskolan* (National curriculum for nine-year compulsory schooling, 1980). Stockholm: Swedish National Agency of Education.

SNSB (1981). *Författningssamling* (School ordinance). Stockholm: Swedish National School Board.

Solmon, M. A. (2014). Physical education, sports, and gender in schools. *Advances in child development and behavior*, *47*, 117-150.

Sundén, J. 2015. "On Trans-, Glitch, and Gender as a Machinery of Failure." *Firstmonday, 20*(4-6).

Svender, J., Larsson, H., & Redelius, K. (2012). Promoting girls' participation in sports: discursive constructions of girls in a sports initiative. *Sport, Education and Society*, *17*(4), 463-478.

Theberge, N. (2006). The gendering of sports injury: A look at 'progress' in women's sport through a case study of the biomedical discourse on the injured athletic body. *Sport in society*, *9*(4), 634-648.

The Swedish Education Act (2014:96). Stockholm: Department of Education.

Thomas, R. (1991). *Histoire du sport*. Paris: Presses Universitaires de France.

Tinning, R., & Fitzclarence, L. (1992). Postmodern youth culture and the crisis in Australian secondary school physical education. *Quest*, *44*(3), 287-303.

Title IX (Education Amendments Act of 1972, 2018). Education Amendments Act of 1972, 20 U.S.C. §§1681 - 1688 (2018).

Veyne, P. (2010). *Foucault: His thought, his character*. Cambridge: Polity.

West, C., & Zimmerman, D. H. (1987). Doing gender. *Gender & society*, *1*(2), 125-151.

Williams, J. F. (1930). Education through the physical. *The Journal of Higher Education*, *1*(5), 279-282.

Wollstonecraft, M. (2004, originally published in 1792). *A Vindication of the Rights of Woman*. Edited by M Brody Kramnick. Harmondsworth: Penguin.

Young, I. M. (1980). Throwing like a girl: A phenomenology of feminine body comportment motility and spatiality. *Human studies*, 137-156.

Electronic sources

Britannica.com/equal-opportunity,
https://www.britannica.com/topic/equal-opportunity

EIGE/sports,
https://eige.europa.eu/topics/sport

HCHR (2019). "Fact sheet: Intersex."
https://unfe.org/system/unfe-65-Intersex_Factsheet_ENGLISH.pdf

www.ingramcontent.com/pod-product-compliance
Lightning Source LLC
Chambersburg PA
CBHW022137160426
43197CB00009B/1324